THE PI

Volume – I

THE PRAYER
OF THE FROG
A BOOK OF STORY MEDITATIONS

Volume – I

Anthony de Mello S.J.

2017
GUJARAT SAHITYA PRAKASH
P.B. 70, ANAND – 388 001
GUJARAT, INDIA

E-mail: booksgsp@gmail.com

Web Site: www.gspbooks.in

1st Edition 1988
18th Edition 2013
19th Edition 2017

ISBN 81-87886-25-0

Price: ₹ 180.00 $15.00

Published by Jerry Sequeira, S.J., Gujarat Sahitya Prakash, P.Box 70,
Anand, Gujarat − 388 001, India.
Printed by Anthony P. Vedam, S.J., Anand Press,
Gamdi-Anand, Gujarat − 388 001, India.

CONTENTS

Foreword XV

Warning XIX

PRAYER

The prayer of the frog 3

The dancing rabbi 4

The ballet prayer 5

Feet pointed to Mecca 6

The prayer of Vishnu's devotee 6

The inventor...7

Become changed into fire 8

The prayer of the cobbler 9

The alphabet prayer...10

God's profession is to forgive 11

Narada carries a milk bowl 12

The village was always helped 13

Can prayer control the weather............................14

Lakshmi's delayed response.................................14

The prayer of children..16

The monumental bore...17

Of prayer and pray-ers 18

Can I help you? 20

Both listen. Neither talks.......................................21

Akbar at namaaz...22

The angry bull 23

Prayer as acceptance of life 24

On a cold day, freeze 24

Making friends with a dragon 25

God is out there 26

The monk and the bird...27

Taking off the blindfold 28
Feet on the desk...28
The forest church..29

AWARENESS

The pillars of religion 33
The three wise men...34
The hunters' flight...35
My Uncle George? 36
Rumour creates a famine 36
The Papal Pantomime 37
The old Jewish lady's conclusion...40
The price of tomatoes 41
The hippy with one shoe..42
The Indian listening to the ground.......................................42
The oyster's misfortune 43
Identifying your mother 44
The dog who walked on water..45
The dog who played cards 46
Grandma's silence 47
The seeker and the devil 48
Blisters on a drunkard's ear..49
The Viennese surgeon's test..50
The parish priest discovers his cook.....................................51
"Get this tramp out of my sight"...52
"One of you is the messiah" 53
The prisoner and the ant 55
El Greco's darkness...55
The blind rabbi...56

RELIGION

The station near the railway tracks 59
The Kamakura Buddha 59
Dov Ber and the Baal Shem...60

The burnt Buddha..61

The invisible sutras..62

Two brothers who loved 63

God will take care of the Messiah!................................65

The hazards of being a chosen people 66

Let go of the branch 67

Lay the blanket on the ground 68

Let God deduct the money in advance 69

Hope in God means no hope..69

Whom would God forgive...70

The experts who opened the Gates of Mercy.................70

How to persue the evil-doer 71

Look directly at the moon...72

The drunkard looks down at the moon 73

The lost motto 74

Where am I..75

Svetaketu's wisdom..76

The menu is not for eating..77

Reading the character called I 77

The Great Revelation 78

A cleric recognize 81

What he is playing is the violin.....................................82

Chicken broth for the dead 83

The conceited non-scholar 84

The Hindu Sage on Jesus 85

The spiritual elite 86

A great revival...87

The resurrected philosopher 88

What is matter made of?...89

The fisherman turned Godman 91

Mary wants to be a Prostitute 93

The rabbi's son became a Christian 94

The rabbi's ecumenical wish..95

The dog and the fox 96

Gandhi turned out of Church 97
God kept out of Church..97
Don't let me catch you praying! 98
You can only cry in your own parish 99
The devil organizes creation 100
The sign of the cross or love? 101
An imprimatur for Jesus..101
How to keep a loin-cloth 102
The life-saving station 103
The fruit commandment 105
The frightened paratrooper..107
Walnut for the rifle butt 108
Railway regulations...109
Telephone exchange regulations 109
Supper must be ready at 6.00 110
Nasruddin finds a diamond 111
Two types of Sabbath 112
Beware, Beware 114

GRACE

Providence in three rescue boats 119
Acquisition and renunciation 120
The earthquake and the drink..121
"Boy, did we shake that bridge!" 121
The old woman and her rooster...122
Tie your camel 123
"The Lord and you are partners".......................................123
Hasan stands guard over a coat 124
God's help in the desert..124
Expectant fathers 125
The official's resolution 125
Don't forget this is America 126
"Put more men on the job"...126
Buying seeds, not fruit..127

"Buy a lottery ticket" 128
Mozart's a advice 129
Stamina in one's old age 129
God plays golf 130
The plumber and Niagara Falls 130

THE SAINTS

No brakes to the fire truck 133
Lady Pumphampton 133
The holy shadow 134
Paul Cezanne 136
Subhuti and emptiness 137
The holy rabbi's modesty 138
The venerable priest pleads guilty 139
The four monks breaks silence 140
The tight halo 141
What's better than a baronetcy? 142
"Look who think he's a sinner!" 142
The punishment of the celibate 143
Thoughts of God and a pretty woman 144
The Master drinks soya bean sauce 145
Nisterus flees the dragon 145
How Longinus healed 146
Bahaudin conceals his miracles 147
Laila and Rama 148
Gessen, the greedy monk 149
The Minister, the rabbi and the priest 151
The bishop's profanity 152
The good-natured Tanzan 153
Glass picker on the beach 155
The somersaulting ascetic 156
The priest who thought ill of on one 157
Rinzai's belly laugh 158
From Action to Laughter 159
Jesus Christ pleads guilty 160

THE SELF

The mystery of the self...163
The greatest modern invention.............................163
The monk and the self 164
The guru and the crocodiles 165
The devil in angel's disguise 166
"Damned good shot!" 166
Mother or girl-friend? 167
"Agatha is eighty-five" 167
The rooster and the farm horse...........................168
The elephant and the flea.....................................169
The workman-and the choir..................................170
The window cleaner...170
The scientist's flaw 171
The cobweb in the turban.....................................172
"This carrot is mine!" 173
Ching makes a bell-frame 174
Who is Maruf Karkhi? 175
Who are you? 176
Who is a hippie? 177
English blank tapes..178
Drop the self, not the flowers 180
The container and the content 181
Uddalaka's lesson 182

LOVE

"I was sure you'd come" 185
The blood transfusion 186
The love of your family..187
What people save first...187
Tears at a funeral..188
Tears for a burning factory...................................188
Yours trousers or your girlfriend...........................189

What we like in others..189

Lucky daughter, unlucky son 190

"All she wants is me."..191

The sweet heart and the expensive watch............191

A requiem for Mr. Turtle 192

Buddha with a blackened nose 193

Fredrick Wilhelm demands love 194

The escaped husband...195

Dogs chained together...195

A princess chained to a slave................................196

My parents might escape 197

Gratitude for a dog 198

The toad in the lawn 199

When the revolution comes 200

Abraham and the God-hating beggar 200

The God who forgets sins......................................201

John the Dwarf accepts a drink............................202

A gift for a complaining mother 203

Get your heart to the mountains 203

Jeremiah and the anvil..204

Al-Mamun's horse 205

Planting trees for posterity 206

The stone in the street...206

How to tell day from night....................................207

The prejudice of Charles Lamb 208

The rabbi who served in secret.............................208

Gandhi's table cloth 209

"I am a bad coin"..210

"She has no family"...211

Anastasius and the stolen bible............................212

The master strikes Jitoku.......................................213

Master Muso's patients 214

The intertwined limbs 215

TRUTH

Life is like a cup of tea 219
A lighter sentence 220
Older housekeepers for priests 220
Naming one's firstborn 221
The price of a bicycle...222
Worker motivation 223
The teddybear theory 224
Nasruddin offers his breath 225
The orchestra conductor's request............................225
No problems, only opportunities 226
An Englishman wins the American Revolution...................227
Those Russian winters 228
A Ph.D. husband's love 229
One horse to one chicken 230
Two percent of the men 230
Fear of mice..231
The greatest man on earth 231
Leg-pain from old age 232
Ping-ting comes for fire 233
Genesha's reply 234
The lighthouse in the porthole 235
The same age for the last ten years 235
"I'm no alien." 236
The audience was a failure..236
The birds sing in South China....................................237
The frog and the ocean..238
The tightrope over the chasm 239
Truth is found in housework......................................240
"You have my marrow." 241
Hui-neng is the successor...241
Don't confuse the jury 242
The knocking in the seeker's heart 243
A Chinese rejection slip...244

Who's doing the leading? 245
Of course you are going to Calcutta 246
A drunk in a cesspool 247
"Dad, I'm back" 248
The father of the victim..248

FOREWORD

The first image of Tony de Mello that I cherish goes back thirty years—and precisely to Lonavla, to the very house that much later became the home of the Sadhana institute.

Tony was then a Jesuit student, but engaged in teaching the young men who had just finished their noviciate. The whole group had come up to St Stanislaus' Villa for a brief holiday. I remember Tony with a batch of juniors, as we called them, sitting under the trees outside the kitchen and cleaning vegetables for the day's meals, whilst he regaled a very receptive audience with his inexhaustible fund of stories.

Much has happened to all of us since then; and Tony himself went through innumerable stages of growth and change, of fresh competence and new interests, and of effective service. But he was always an incomparable story-teller. Hardly any of his anecdotes were original, and some were not even exceptionally smart; but on his lips they came alive with meaning and relevance, or just plain fun. For that matter, any theme he touched came alive and captured attention.

And now his parting gift to us, which will surely join the ranks of his other best-sellers, is The Prayer of the Frog. Though he spoke rather casually of his literary output, he was meticulous in editing his compositions. The last thing he did in India before taking the plane for the United States, was to spend more than three hours with the publisher, going over the details of his manuscript. I have not seen the text, but I know of his final concern.

That was in the evening of May 30th, 1987. On June 2nd he was found dead on the floor of his room in New York, having succumbed to a massive heart attack. In between he had made time to write a long letter to a close friend, in which he said, speaking of earlier experiences: "All of that seems to belong to another era and to another world. I find the whole of my interest is now focussed on something else, on the 'world of the spirit', and I see everything else as so trifling and so irrelevant. The thing that mattered so much in the past do not seem to matter any more. Things like those of Achaan Chah, the Buddhist teacher, seem to absorb my whole interest and I am losing my taste for other things. Is this an illusion? I do not know. But never before in my life have I felt so happy, so free."

That just about sums up Tony as he was—and indeed as others perceived him—in his last phase, before he left us so suddenly, three months before his fifty-sixth birthday. And now there is already a body of literature that is growing around him, a veritable golden legend, with testimonies from a variety of people scattered the world over. Quite a few have said they never met him but were profoundly affected by his books. Others had enjoyed the privilege of a deep relationship. Yet others only briefly experienced the magic of his spoken word.

Not many would go along with everything that he said or did, especially after he crossed the established boundaries of spiritual venture—nor did Tony expect a docile following, but rather the contrary. What attracted so many to his person and ideas was precisely that he challenged everyone to question, to explore, to get out of prefabricated patterns of though and behaviour, away from stereotypes, and to dare be one's true self—in fine, to seek an ever greater authenticity.

A relentless quest for authenticity—that is how Tony's vision came across from any angle, at any range. And this gave to his multifaceted personality an integrity, a wholeness, that had a charm and a power all its own: it reconciled opposites, not in tension but as a harmonious blend. He was most ready to make friends, to share; yet one felt there was a dimension in him that was out of reach. He could be boisterous in company, trotting out outrageous jokes, but no one could doubt his steadfast seriousness of purpose. He changed so much and in so many ways along the years, and nevertheless there were constants in his character that stayed firmly in place.

A striking example of this was his commitment as a Jesuit. He had moved far beyond the enthusiastic promotion of the Spiritual Exercises according to the original design of Saint Ignatius—which was the thrust for which he first came to be internationally appreciated; in fact, at the end he was way out of what might be recognized as Ignatian spirituality. But he never surrendered his Jesuit identity. There was obviously no compulsion in this; probably not much reasoning either. It was just that he felt so much in tune with the mind and heart of Ignatius, as he knew and understood the Saint.

In a homily that he addressed to the Jesuit Provincials of India in 1983, before they and he himself participated in the last General Congregation, or Chapter of the Order, he shared with them an insight into Ignatius which was even more a self-revelation of Tony:

"There is a tradition among our early Fathers that God gave to Ignatius the graces and charisms that He intended for the Society as a whole and for each individual Jesuit. If I were asked to choose for myself and for our Society today from among the many charisms that Ignatius had, I would quite unhesitatingly choose three: his contemplation, his creativity and his courage."

Parmananda R. Divarkar S.J.

4th September, 1987

WARNING

It is a great mystery that though the human heart longs for Truth in which alone it finds liberation and delight, the first reaction of human beings to Truth is one of hostility and fear. So the Spiritual Teachers of humanity, like Buddha and Jesus, created a device to circumvent the opposition of their listeners: the story. They knew that the most entrancing words a language holds are, "One upon a time...", that it is common to oppose a truth but impossible to resist a story. Vyasa, the author of the Mahabharata, says that if you listen carefully to a story you will never be the same again. That is because the story will worm its way into your heart and break down barriers to the divine. Even if you read the stories in this book only for the entertainment there is no guarantee that an occasional story will not slip through your defences and explode when you least expect it to. So you have been warned!

If you are foolhardy enough to court enlightenment, this is what I suggest you do:

> *(A) Carry a story around in your mind so you can dwell on it in leisure moments. That will give it a chance to work on your subconscious and reveal its hidden meaning. You will then be surprised to see how it comes to you quite unexpectedly just when you need it to light up an event or situation and bring you insight and inner healing. That is when you will realize that, in exposing yourself to these stories, you were auditing a Course in Enlightenment for which no guru is needed other than yourself!*

> *(B) Since each of these stories is a revelation of Truth and since Truth, when spelt with a capital T, means the truth about you, make sure that each time you read a story you single-mind-edly search for a deeper understanding of yourself. The way one would read a Medical Book—wondering if one has any of the symptoms; and one's friends are. If you succumb to the temptation of seeking insight into others, the stories will do you damage.*

So passionate was Mulla Nasruddin's love for truth that he travelled to distant places in search of Koranic scholars and he felt no inhibitions about drawing infidels at the bazaar into discussions about the truths of his faith.'

One day his wife told him how unfairly he was treating her—and discovered that her husband had no interest whatsoever in that kind of Truth!

It's the only kind that matters, of course. Ours would be a different would, indeed, if those of us who are scholars and ideologues, whether religious or secular, had the same passion for self-knowledge that we display for our theories and dogmas.

*   *   *   *   *

"Excellent sermon," said the parishioner, as she pumped the hand of the preacher. "Everything you said applies to someone or other I know."

See?

INSTRUCTION

The stories are best read in the order in which they are set out here. Read no more than one or two at a time—that is, if you wish to get anything more than entertainment from them.

NOTE

The stories in this book come from a variety of countries, cultures and religions. They belong to the spiritual heritage—and popular humour—of the human race.

All that the author has done is string them together with a specific aim in mind. His task has been that of the weaver and the dyer. He takes no credit at all for the cotton and the thread.

PRAYER

PRAYER

When Brother Bruno was at prayer one night he was disturbed
by the crocking of a bullfrog. All the attempts to disregard
the sound were unsuccessful so he shouted from his window,
"Quiet! I'm at my prayers."

Now Brother Bruno was a saint so his command was instantly
obeyed. Every living creature held its voice so as to create a
silence that would be favourable to prayer.

But now another sound intruded on Bruno's worship— an inner
voice that said, "Maybe God is as pleased with the croaking
of that frog as with the chanting of your psalms." "What can
please the ears of God in the croak of a frog?" was Bruno's
scornful rejoinder. But the voice refused to give up: "Why would
you think God invented the sound?"

Bruno decided to find out why. He leaned out of his window
and gave the order, "Sing!" The bullfrog's measured croaking
filled the air to the ludicrous accompaniment of all the frogs in
the vicinity. And as Bruno attended to the sound, their voices
ceased to jar for he discovered that, if he stopped resisting
them, they actually enriched the silence of the night.

With that discovery Bruno's heart became harmonious with the
universe and, for the first time in his life he understood what it
means to pray.

A Hasidic tale:

The Jews of a small town in Russia were eagerly awaiting the arrival of a Rabbi. This was going to be a rare event so they spent a lot of time preparing the questions they were going to put to the holy man.

When he finally arrived and they met with him in the town hall, he could sense the tension in the atmosphere as all prepared to listen to the answers he had for them.

He said nothing at first; he just gazed into their eyes, and hummed a haunting melody. Soon everyone began to hum. He started to sing and they sang along with him. He swayed and danced in solemn, measured steps. The congregation followed suit. Soon they became so involved in the dance, so absorbed in its movements that they were lost to everything else on earth; so every person in that crowd was made whole, was healed from the inner fragmentation that keeps us from the Truth.

It was nearly an hour before the dance slowed down to a halt. With the tension drained out of their inner being everyone sat in the silent peace that pervaded the room. Then the Rabbi spoke the only words he pronounced that evening: "I trust that I have answered your questions."

A dervish was asked why he worshipped God through dance. "Because," he replied, "to worship God means to die to self; dancing kills the self. When the self dies all problems die with it. Where the self is not, Love is, God is."

The Master sat with his disciples in the audience. He said. "You have *heard* many a prayer and *said* many a prayer. Tonight I should like you to see one."

At that moment the curtain rose and the ballet began.

A Sufi saint set out on a pilgrimage to Mecca. At the outskirts of the city he lay down by the road, exhausted from his journey. He had barely fallen asleep when he brusquely awakened by an irate pilgrim. "This is the time when all believers bow their heads towards Mecca and you have your feet pointing towards the holy shrine. What sort of Muslim are you?"

The Sufi did not move; he merely opened his eyes and said, "Brother, would you do me the favour of placing my feet where they won't be pointing to the Lord?"

The prayer of a devotee to the Lord Vishnu:

"Lord, I ask you to pardon me for three major sins: first, I went on pilgrimage to your many shrines, oblivious of your presence everywhere; second, I so often cried to you for help, forgetting that you are more concerned than I am about my welfare; and finally, here I am asking for forgiveness when I know that our sins are forgiven before we commit them."

After many years of labour an inventor discovered the art of making fire. He took his tools to the snow-clad northern regions and initiated a tribe into the art—and the advantages—of making fire. The people became so absorbed in this novelty that it did not occur to them to thank the inventor who one day quietly slipped away. Being one of those rare human beings endowed with greatness, he had no desire to be remembered or revered; all he sought was the satisfaction of knowing that someone had benefitted from his discovery.

The next tribe he went to was just as eager to learn as the first. But the local priests, jealous of the stranger's hold on the people, had him assassinated. To allay any suspicion of the crime, they had a portrait of the Great Inventor enthroned upon the main altar of the temple; and a liturgy designed so that his name would be revered and his memory kept alive. The greatest care was taken that not a single rubric of the liturgy was altered or omitted. The tools for making fire were enshrined within a casket and were said to bring healing to all who laid their hands on them with faith.

The High Priest himself undertook the task of compiling a Life of the Inventor. This became the Holy book in which his loving kindness was offered as an example for all to emulate, his glorious deeds were eulogized, his superhuman nature made an article of faith. The priests saw to it that the Book was handed down to future generations, while they authoritatively interpreted the meaning of his words and the significance of his holy life and death. And they ruthlessly punished with death or excommunication anyone who deviated from their doctrine. Caught up as they were in these religious tasks, the people completely forgot the art of making fire.

From the Lives of the Desert Fathers:

Abbot Lot came to abbot Joseph and said, "Father, according to my capacity I keep my little rule and my little fast, my prayer, my meditation, my contemplative silence; and according as I am able I cleanse my heart of evil thoughts. Now what more should I do?"

The elder stood up in reply. He stretched out his hand to heaven and his fingers became like ten lamps of fire. He said: "This: become totally changed into fire."

PRAYER

A cobbler came to Rabbi Issac of Ger and said, "Tell me what to do about my morning prayer. My customers are poor men who have only one pair of shoes. I pick up their shoes late in the evening and work on them most of the night; at dawn there is still work to be done if the men are to have their shoes ready before they go to work. Now my question is: What should I do about my morning prayer?"

"What have you been doing till now?" the Rabbi asked.

"Sometimes I rush through the prayer quickly and get back to my work–but then I feel bad about it. At other times I let the hour of prayer go by. Then too I feel a sense of loss and every now and then as I raise my hammer from the shoes. I can almost hear my heart sigh. 'What and unlucky man I am, that I am not able to make my morning prayer."

Said the Rabbi, "If I were God I would value that sigh more than the prayer."

A Hasidic tale:

Late one evening a poor farmer on his way back from the market found himself without his prayer book. The wheel of his cart had come off right in the middle of the woods and it distressed him that this day should pass without his having said his prayers.

So this is the prayer he made: "I have done something very foolish, Lord. I came away from home this morning without my prayer book and my memory is such that I cannot recite a single prayer without it. So this is what I am going to do: I shall recite the alphabet five times very slowly and you, to whom all prayers are known, can put the letters together to form the prayers I can't remember."

And the Lord said to his angels, "Of all the prayers I have heard today, this one was undoubtedly the best because it came from a heart that was simple and sincere."

It is the Custom among Catholics to confess their sins to a priest and receive absolution from him as a sign of God's forgiveness. Now all too often there is the danger that penitents will use this as a sort of guarantee, a certificate that will protect them from divine retribution, thereby placing more trust in the absolution of the priest than in the mercy of God.

This is what Perugini, an Italian painter of the Middle Ages, was tempted to do when he was dying. He decided that he would not go to confession if, in his fear, he was seeking to save his skin. That would be a sacrilege and an insult to God.

His wife, who knew nothing of the man's inner disposition, once asked him if he did not fear to die unconfessed. Perugini replied: "Look at it this way, my dear: My profession is to paint and I have excelled as a painter. God's profession is to forgive and if he is good at his profession as I have been at mine, I see no reason to be afraid."

The Indian sage, Narada, was a devotee of the Lord Hari. So great was his devotion that he was one day tempted to think that in all the world there was no one who loved God more than he.

The Lord read his heart and said, "Narada, go to this town on the banks of the Ganges for a devotee of mine dwells there. Living in his company will do you good."

Narada went and found a farmer who rose early in the morning, pronounced the name of Hari only once, then lifted his plough and went out to his fields where he worked all day. Just before he fell asleep at night he pronounced the name of Hari once again. Narada thought, "How can this rustic be a devotee of God? I see him immersed all day in his worldly occupations."

Then the Lord said to Narada, "Fill a bowl to the brim with milk and walk all round the city. Then come back without spilling a single drop." Narada did as he was told.

"How many times did you remember me in the course of your walk around the city?" asked the Lord.'

"Not once, Lord," said Narada. "How could I when you commanded me to watch that bowl of milk?"

The Lord said, "That bowl so absorbed your attention that you forgot me altogether. But look at that peasant who, though burdened with the cares of supporting a family, remembers me twice every day?"

PRAYER

The village priest was a holy man so each time the people were in trouble they had recourse to him. He would then withdraw to a special place in the forest and say a special prayer. God would always hear his prayer and the village would be helped.

When he died and the people were in trouble they had recourse to his successor who was not a holy man but knew the secret of the special place in the forest and the special prayer. So he said, "Lord, you know I am not a holy man. But surely you are not going to hold that against my people? So listen to my prayer and come to our assistance." And God would hear his prayer and the village would be helped.

When he too died and the people were in trouble they had recourse to his successor who knew the special prayer but not the place in the forest. So he said, "What do you care for places, Lord? Is not every place made holy by your presence? So listen to my prayer and come to out assistance." And once again God would hear his prayer and the village would be helped.

Now he too died and when the people were in trouble they had recourse to his successor who did not know the special prayer or the special place in the forest. So he said, "It isn't the formula that you value, Lord, but the cry of the heart in distress. So listen to my prayer and come to our assistance." And once again God would hear his prayer and the village would be helped.

After this man died when the people were in trouble they had recourse to his successor. Now this priest had more use for money than for prayer. So he would say to God, "What sort of a God are you that while you are perfectly capable of solving problems that you yourself have caused, you still refuse to lift a finger until you have us cringe and beg and plead? Well, you can do as you please with the people." Then he would go right back to whatever business he had in hand. And, once again, God would hear his prayer and the village would be helped.

An elderly woman who was an enthusiastic gardener declared that she had so faith whatsoever in predictions that some day scientists would learn to control the weather. According to her all that was needed to control the weather was prayer.

Then one summer, while she was away on a foreign trip, a drought hit the land and wiped out her entire garden. She was so upset when she got back that she changed her religion.

She should have changed her silly beliefs.

It's no good having our prayers answered
If they are not answered at the right time:

In ancient India much store was set by the Vedic rites which were said to be so scientific in their application that when the sages prayed for rain there was never any drought. It is thus that a man set himself to pray, according to these rites, to the goddess of wealth, Lakshmi, begging her to make him rich.

He prayed to no effect for ten long years, after which period of time, he suddenly saw the illusory nature of wealth and adopted the life of a renunciate in the Himalayas.

He was sitting in meditation one day when he opened
his eyes and saw before him an extra-ordinarily beautiful
woman, all bright and shining as if she were made of
gold.

"Who are you and what are you doing here?" he asked.

"I am the goddess Lakshmi to whom you recited hymns for
twelve years," said the woman. "I have appeared to grant
you your desire."

"Ah, my dear goddess," exclaimed the man, "I have since
attained the bliss of meditation and lost my desire for
wealth. You come too late. Tell me, why did you delay so
long in coming?"

"To tell you the truth," said the goddess, "Given the nature
of those rites you so faithfully performed you had fully
earned the wealth. But, in my love for you and my desire
for your welfare, I held it back."

If you had the choice, which would you choose:
the granting of your petition
or the grace to be peaceful
whether it is granted or not?

One day Mulla Nasruddin saw the village schoolmaster leading a group of children towards the mosque.

"What are you taking them there for?" he asked.

"There is a drought in the land," said the teacher, "and we trust that the cries of the innocent will move the heart of the Almighty."

"It isn't the cries, whether innocent or criminal, that count," said the Mulla, "But wisdom and awareness."

"How dare you make such a blasphemous statement in the presence of these children!" cried the teacher. "Prove what you have said, or you shall be denounced as a heretic."

"Easy enough," said Nasruddin. "If the prayers of children counted for anything there wouldn't be a school teacher in all the land, for there is nothing they so detest as going to school. The reason you have survived those prayers is that we, who know better than the children, have kept you where you are?"

A pious old man prayed five times a day while his business partner never set foot in church. And now, on his eightieth birthday he prayed thus:

"Oh Lord our God! Since I was a youth not a day have I allowed to pass without coming to church in the morning and saying my prayers at the five specified times. Not a single move, not one decision, important or trifling did I make without first invoking your Name. And now, in my old age, I have doubled my exercises of piety and pray to you ceaselessly, night and day. Yet here I am, poor as a church mouse. But look at my business partner. He drinks and gambles and, even at his advanced age, consorts with women of questionable character yet he's rolling in wealth. I wonder if a single prayer has ever crossed his lips. Now, Lord, I do not ask that he be punished, for that would be unchristian. But please tell me: Why, have you let him prosper and why do you treat me thus?"

"Because," said God in reply, "you are such a monumental bore!"

The Rule in a monastery was not, "Do not speak," but, "Do not speak unless you can improve on the silence."

Might not the same be said of prayer?

Of *prayers and pray-ers:*

> Grandmother: "Do you say your prayer every night?"
> Grandson: "Oh, yes!"
> "And every morning?"
> "No. I'm not scared in the daytime."

Pious old lady, after the war: "God was very good to us. We prayed and prayed, so all the bombs fell on the other side of the town!"

PRAYER

So intolerable had Hitler's persecution of the Jews become that two Jews decided to assassinate him. They mounted guard, their guns at the ready, at a spot by which they knew the Fuehrer was to pass. He was long in coming and a horrible thought occurred to Samuel. "Joshua," he said, "say a prayer that nothing's happened to the man!"

They had made it their custom to invite their pious aunt to go with them on their picnic each year. This year they forgot. When the invitation did come at the last minute, she said, "It's too late now. I've already prayed for rain."

A priest observed a woman sitting in the empty church with her head in her hands.

An hour passed. Then two. Still she was there.'

Judging her to be a soul in distress, and eager to be of assistance, he went up to the woman and said, "Is there any way I can be of help?"

"No, thank you, Father," She said. "I've been getting all the help I need."

Until you interrupted!

An old man would sit motionless for hours on end in church. One day a priest asked him what god talked to him about!

"God doesn't talk. He just listens," was his reply.

"Well, then what do you talk to him about?"

"I don't talk either. I just listen."

The four stages of Prayer:
I talk, you listen.
You talk, I listen.
Neither talks, both listen.
Neither talks, neither listens: Silence

The Sufi Bayazid Bistami describes his progress in the art of prayer: "The first time I visited the Kaaba at Mecca, I saw the Kaaba. The second time I saw the Lord of the Kaaba. The third time I saw neither the Kaaba nor the Lord of the Kaaba."

The Moghul Emperor, Akbar, was one day out hunting
in the forest. When it was time for evening prayer he
dismounted, spread his mat on the earth and knelt to pray
in the manner of devout Muslims everywhere.

Now it was precisely at this time a peasant woman,
perturbed by the disappearance of her husband who
had left home that morning and hadn't returned, went
rushing by, anxiously searching for her husband. In her
preoccupation she did not notice the kneeling figure of the
Emperor and tripped over him, then got up and without a
word of apology rushed further into the forest.

Akbar was annoyed at this interruption but, being a good
Muslim, he observed the rule of speaking to no one during
the namaaz.

Now just about the time that his prayer was over the
woman returned, joyful in the company of her husband
whom she had found. She was surprised and frightened
to see the Emperor and his entourage there. Akbar gave
vent to his anger against her and shouted, "Explain your
disrespectful behaviour or you will be punished."

The woman suddenly turned fearless, looked into the
Emperor's eyes and said, "Your Majesty, I was so absorbed
in the though of my husband that I did not even see you
here, not even when, as you say, I stumbled over you. Now
while you were at namaaz, you were absorbed in One
who is infinitely more precious than my husband. And how
is it you noticed me?"

The Emperor was shamed into silence and later confided
to his friends that a peasant woman, who was neither a
scholar nor a Mullah, had taught him the meaning of
prayer.

PRAYER

Once the Master was at prayer. The disciples came up to him and said, "Sir, teach us how to pray." This is how he taught them...

Two men were once walking through a field when they saw an angry bull. Instantly they made for the nearest fence with the bull in hot pursuit. It soon became evident to them that they were not going to make it, so one man shouted to the other, "We've had it! Nothing can save us. Say a prayer. Quick!"

The other shouted back, "I've never prayed in my life and I don't have a prayer for this occasion."

"Never mind. The bull is catching up with us. Any prayer will do."

"Well, I'll say the one I remember my father used to say before meals: For what we are about to receive, Lord, make us truly grateful."

Nothing surpasses the holiness of those
who have learnt perfect acceptance
of everything that is.

In the game of cards called life
one plays the hand one is dealt
to the best of one's ability.

Those who insist on playing,
not the hand they were given
but the one they insist they should have been dealt
—these are life's failures.

We are not asked if we will play.
That is not an option. Play we must
The option is how.

A rabbi once asked a pupil what was bothering him.

"My poverty," was the reply. "So wretched is my condition that I can hardly study and pray."

"In this day and age," said the rabbi, "the finest prayer and the finest study lie in accepting life exactly as you find it."

On a bitterly cold day a rabbi and his disciples were huddled around a fire.

One of the disciples echoing his master's teachings, said, "On a freezing day like this I know exactly what to do!"
"What?" asked the others.
"Keep warm! And if that isn't possible, I still know what to do."
"What?"
"Freeze."

Present Reality cannot really
be rejected or accepted.
To run away from it
is like running away from your feet.
To accept it
is like kissing your lips.
All you need to do is see, understand,
and be at rest.

A man went to see a psychiatrist and said that every night he was visited by a twelve-foot dragon with three heads. He was a nervous wreck, could not sleep at all and was on the verge of total collapse. He had even thought of suicide.

"I think I can help you," said the psychiatrist, "but I must warn you that it will take a year or two and will cost three thousand dollars."

"Three thousand dollars!" the man exclaimed. "Forget it! I'll just go home and make friends with it."

The Muslim mystic, Farid, was prevailed upon by his neighbours to go to the court in Delhi and obtain a favour from Akbar for the Village. Farid walked into the court and found Akbar at his prayers:

When the Emperor finally emerged, Farid asked. "What sort of prayer did you make?"

"I prayed that the All-Merciful would bestow success and wealth and long life on me," was the reply.

Farid promptly turned his back on the Emperor and walked away, remarking, "I came to see an Emperor. What I find here is a beggar no different from the rest!"

There was once a woman who was religious and devout and filled with love for God. Each morning she would go to Church. And on her way children would call out to her, beggars would accost her, but so immersed was she in her devotions that she did not even see them.

Now one day she walked down the street in her customary manner and arrived at the church just in time for service. She pushed the door, but it would not open. She pushed it again harder, and found the door was locked.

Distressed at the thought that she would miss service for the first time in years, and not knowing what to do, she looked up. And there, right before her face, she found a note pinned on to the door.

It said, "I'm out there!"

Of a saint it used to be said that each time he left home to go and perform his religious duties he would say, "And now, Lord, good-bye! I am off to Church."

PRAYER

A monk was walking in the monastery grounds one day when he heard a bird sing.

He listened, spellbound. It seemed to him that never before had he heard, but really heard, the song of a bird.

When the singing stopped he returned to the monastery and discovered, to his dismay, that he was a stranger to his fellow monks, and they to him.

It was only gradually that they and he discovered that he was returning after centuries. Because his listening was total, time had stopped and he had slipped into eternity.

Prayer is made perfect
when the timeless is discovered.
The timeless is discovered
through clarity of perception.
Perception is made clear
when it is disengaged
from preconceptions
and from all consideration
of personal loss or gain.
Then the miraculous
is seen and the heart is filled with wonder.

When the Master invited the Governor to practise meditation and the Governor said he was too busy, this is the reply he got:

"You put me in mind of a man walking blind-folded into the jungle—and too busy to take the blindfold off."

When the Governor pleaded lack of time, the Master said, "It is a mistake to think that meditation cannot be practised for lack of time. The real cause is agitation of the mind."

An efficiency expert was making his report to Henry Ford. "As you well see, sir, the report is highly favourable, except for that man down the hall. Every time I pass by he's sitting with his feet on his desk. He's wasting your money.

Said Ford, "That man once had an idea that earned us a fortune. At the time I believe his feet were exactly where they are now."

There was an exhausted woodcutter who kept wasting time and energy chopping wood with a blunt axe because he did not have the time, he said, to stop and sharpen the blade.

Once upon a time there was a forest where the birds sang by day and the insects by night. Trees flourished, flowers bloomed and all manner of creatures roamed about in freedom.

And all who entered there were led to Solitude which is the home of God who dwells in Nature's silence and Nature's beauty.

But then the Age of Unconsciousness arrived when it became possible for people to construct buildings a thousand feet high and to destroy rivers and forests and mountains in a month. So houses of worship were built from the wood of the forest trees and from the stone under the forest soil. Pinnacle, spire and minaret pointed towards the sky; the air was filled with the sound of bells, with prayer and chant and exhortation.

And God was suddenly without a home.

God hides things by putting them before our eyes!

Hark! Listen to the song of the bird,
the wind in the trees,
the ocean roar;
look at a tree, a falling leaf, a flower
as if for the first time.

You might suddenly make contact
with Reality
with that Paradise
from which we,
having fallen from childhood,
are excluded by our knowledge.

Says the Indian mystic Saraha:
"Know the taste of this flavour
Which is the absence of Knowledge."

AWARENESS

A great religious persecution broke out in the land and the three Pillars of religion, Scripture, Worship and Charity appeared before God to express their fear that, if religion was stamped out, they would cease to exist.

"Not to worry," said the Lord, "I plan to send One to earth who is greater than all of you."

"By what name is this Great One called?"

"Self-knowledge," said God. "He will do greater things than any of you have done."

Three wise men set out on a journey for, even though they were considered wise in their own country, they were humble enough to hope that travel would broaden their minds.

They had barely crossed into a neighbouring country when they saw a skyscraper in the distance. What could this enormous object be, they asked themselves? The obvious answer would have been: go up and find out. But no, that might be too dangerous. Suppose it was something that exploded as one approached? It was altogether wiser to decide what it was before finding out. Various theories were put forward, examined and, on the basis of their past experience, rejected. Finally, it was determined, also on the basis of past experience of which they had an abundant supply, that the object in question, whatever it was, could only have been placed there by giants.

This led them to the conclusion that it would be safer to avoid this country altogether. So they went back home having added something to their fund of experience.

Assumptions affect Observation.
Observation breeds Conviction.
Conviction produces Experience.
Experience generates Behaviour.
which, in turn, confirms Assumptions.

Assumptions:

A couple of hunters chartered a plane to fly them into forest territory. Two weeks later the pilot came to take them back. He took a look at the animals they had shot and said, "This plane won't take more than one wild buffalo. You'll have to leave the other behind."

"But last year the pilot let us take two in a plane this size," the hunters protested.

The pilot was doubtful, but finally he said, "Well, if you did it last year I guess we can do it again."

So the plane took off with the three men and two buffaloes. But it couldn't gain height and crashed into a neighbouring hill. The men climbed out and looked around. One hunter said to the other, "Where do you think we are?" The other inspected the surroundings and said, "I think we're about two miles to the left of where we crashed last year."

And more assumptions:

A married couple was returning from the funeral of Uncle George who had lived with them for twenty years and had been such a nuisance that he almost succeeded in wrecking their marriage.

"There is something I have to say to you, dear," said the man. "If it hadn't been for my love for you I wouldn't have put up with your Uncle George for a single day."

"My Uncle George!" she exclaimed in horror. "I thought he was *your* Uncle George!"

In the summer of 1946 the rumour of a famine swept through a province in a South American country. Actually the crops were growing well, and the weather was perfect for a bumper harvest. But on the strength of that rumour 20,000 small farmers abandoned their farms and fled to the cities. Because of their action the crops failed, thousands starved and the rumour about the famine proved true.

AWARENESS

Many, many years ago, back in the Middle Ages, the Pope
was urged by his advisors to banish the Jews from Rome. It
was unseemly, they said, that these people should be living
unmolested in the very centre of Catholicism. An edict of
eviction was drawn up and promulgated much to the dismay
of they Jews who knew that wherever else they went they could
only expect worse treatment than was meted out to them
in Rome. So they pleaded with the Pope to reconsider the
edict. The Pope, a fair-minded man, offered them a sporting
proposition: Let the Jews appoint someone to debate with him
in pantomime. It their spokesman won the Jews might stay.

The Jews met to consider this proposal. To turn it down was
to be evicted from Rome. To accept it was to court certain
defeat, for who could win a debate in which the Pope was
both participant and judge? Still, there was nothing for it but to
accept. Only, it was impossible to find someone to volunteer for
the task of debating with the Pope. The burden of having the
fate of the Jews on his shoulders was more than anyone man
could bear.

Now when the synagogue janitor heard what was going on, he
came before the Chief Rabbi and volunteered to represent his
people in the debate. "The janitor?" said the other rabbis when
they heard of this. "Impossible!"

"Well," said the Chief Rabbi, "None of us is willing. It is either
the janitor or no debate." Thus for lack of anyone else the janitor was appointed to debate with the Pope.

When the great day arrived, the Pope sat on a throne in St Peter's square surrounded by his cardinals, facing a large crowd

37

of bishops, priests and faithful. Presently the little Jewish delegation arrived in their black robes and flowing beards, with the
janitor in their midst.

The Pope turned to face the janitor ad the debate began.
The Pope solemnly raised one finger and traced it across the
heavens. The janitor promptly pointed with emphasis towards
the ground. The Pope seemed somewhat taken aback. Even
more solemnly he raised one finger again and kept it firmly
before the Janitor's face. The janitor thereupon lifted three
fingers and held them just as firmly before the Pope who
seemed astonished by the gesture. Then the Pope thrust his
hand into his robes and pulled out an apple. Whereupon the
janitor thrust his hand into his paper bag and pulled out a flat
piece of matzo. At this the Pope explained in a loud voice, "The
Jewish representative has won the debate. The edict of eviction
is hereby revoked."

The Jewish leaders promptly surrounded the janitor and
led him away. The cardinals clustered around the Pope in
astonishment. "What happened, your Holiness?" they asked.
"It was impossible for us to follow the rapid thrust and parry of
the debate." The Pope wiped the sweat from his fore-head and
said, "That man is a brilliant theologian, a master in debate.

I began by sweeping my hand across the sky to indicate that the
whole universe belongs to God. He thrust his finger downward
to remind me that there is a place called Hell where the devil
reigns supreme. I then raised one finger to signify that God is
one. Imagine my shock when he raised three fingers to indicate
that this one God manifests Himself equally in three persons,
thereby subscribing to our own doctrine of the Trinity! Knowing that it was impossible to get the better of this theological
genius I finally shifted the debate to another area. I pulled out
an apple to indicate that according to some new-fangled ideas

the earth is round. He instantly produced a flat piece of unleavened bread to remind me that, according to the Bible, the earth is flat. So there was nothing to do but concede the victory to him."

By now the Jews had arrived at their synagogue. "What happened they asked the janitor in bewilderment. The janitor was indignant. "It was all a lot of rubbish," he said. "Look. First the Pope moves his hand like he is telling all the Jews to get out of Rome. So I pointed downwards to make it clear to him that we were not going to budge. So he points a finger to me threateningly as if to say. Don't get fresh with me. So I point three fingers to tell him he was thrice as fresh with us when he arbitrarily ordered us out of Rome. The next thing, I see him taking out his lunch. So I took out mine."

Reality, mostly, is not what it is
but what we have decided it is:

A little old Jewish lady sits down in a plane next to a big Swede and keeps staring at him. Finally she turns to him and says, "Pardon me, are you Jewish?"

He says, "No."

A few minutes later she turns to him again and says, "You can tell me, you know—you are Jewish, aren't you?"

He says, "Most certainly not."

She keeps studying him for some minutes, then says again, "I can tell you are Jewish."

In order to get rid of the annoyance the man says, "OK., so I'm Jewish!"

She looks at him again, shakes her head and says, "You certainly don't look it."

We first make our conclusions'
– then find some way to arrive at them.

A woman in the grocery department of a supermarket bent down to pick up some tomatoes. At that moment she felt a sharp pain shooting down her back; she became immobilized and let out a shriek.

A shopper standing next to her leaned over knowingly and said, "If you think tomatoes are bad, you should see the price of the fish!"

Is it Reality you are responding to
or your assumptions about it?

A man got into a bus and found himself sitting next to a youngster who was obviously a hippy. He was wearing only one shoe.

"You've evidently lost a shoe, son."

"No man," came the reply. "I found one."

It is evident to me;
that does not mean it is true.'

A cowboy was riding across the desert when he came upon an Indian lying on the road with his head and ear to the ground.

"How yah doin," chief?" said the cowboy.

"Big paleface with red hair driving dark green Mercedes-Benz with German shepherd dog inside and license plate number SDT965 going headed West."

"Gee, chief, yah mean you hear all that just listening to the ground?"

"I'm not listening to the ground. The SOB ran over me."

An oyster saw a loose pearl that had fallen into the crevice of a rock on the ocean bed. After great effort she managed to retrieve the pearl and place it just beside her on a leaf.

She knew that humans searched for pearls and thought, "This pearl will tempt them, so they will take it and let me be."

When a pearl diver showed up, however, his eyes were conditioned to look for oysters and not for pearls resting on leaves.

So he grabbed the oyster which did not happen to have a pearl and allowed the real pearl to roll back into the crevice in the rock.

You know exactly where to look.
That is the reason why
you fall to find God.

A woman at a bank asked the cashier to cash a cheque for her.

Citing company policy the cashier asked her for identification.

The woman gasped. Finally, she managed to say, "But Jonathan, I'm your mother!"

If you think this is funny,
how come you fail yourself
to recognize the messiah?

AWARENESS

A man took his new hunting dog out on a trial hunt. Presently he shot a duck that fell into the lake. The dog walked over the water, picked the duck up and brought it to his master.

The man was flabbergasted! He shot another duck. Once again, while he rubbed his eyes in disbelief, the dog walked over the water and retrieved the duck.

Hardly daring to believe what he had seen, he called his neighbour for a shoot the following day. Once again, each time he or his neighbour hit a bird the dog would walk over the water and bring the bird in. The man said nothing. Neither did his neighbour. Finally, unable to contain himself any longer, he blurted out, "Did you notice anything strange about that dog?"

The neighbour rubbed his chin pensively. "Yes," he finally said. "Come to think of it, I did! The son of a gun can't swim!"

It isn't as if life is not full of miracles.
It's more than that: it is miraculous,
and anyone who stops taking it for granted
will see it at once.

"That's clever dog you have there," said a man when he saw his friend playing cards with his dog.

"Not as clever as he looks," was the reply. "Every time he gets a good hand he wags his tail."

Grandpa and grandma had quarrelled and grandma was so angry she would not speak to her husband.

The following day grandpa had forgotten all about the quarrel, but grandma continued to ignore him and still wouldn't speak. Nothing grandpa did seem to succeed in pulling her out of her sullen silence.

Finally he started rummaging in cupboards and drawers. After this had gone on for a few minutes, grandma could stand it no longer. "What on earth are you looking for?" she demanded angrily.

"Praised be God, I've found it," said grandpa with a sly smile. "Your voice!"

If it is God you are looking for, look somewhere else.

When the devil saw a seeker enter the house of a Master he determined to do everything in his power to turn him back from his quest for Truth.

So he subjected the poor man to every possible temptation: wealth, lust, fame, power, prestige. But the seeker was far too experienced in spiritual matters and was able to fight off the temptations quite easily, so great was his longing for spirituality.

When he got into the Master's presence, he was somewhat taken aback to see the Master sitting on an upholstered chair and the disciples at his feet. "This man certainly lacks the principal virtue of the saints, humility," he thought to himself.

He then observed other things about the Master that he did not like: for one thing, the Master took little notice of him. ("I suppose that is because I do not fawn on him as the others do," he said to himself). Also the kind of clothes the Master wore and the somewhat conceited way he spoke. All of this led him to the conclusion that he had come to the wrong place and must continue his quest elsewhere.

As he walked out of the room, the Master, who had seen the devil seated in a corner of the room, said, "You need not have worried Tempter. He was yours from the very first, you know."

Such is the fate of those who,
in their search for God,
are willing to shed everything
except their notions of what God really is.

AWARENESS

People would never sin
if they were aware
that each time they sin
it is themselves they are damaging.
Most people are in too much of a torpor, alas,
to have the slightest awareness
of what they are doing to themselves.

A drunkard was walking down a street with blisters in both of his ears. A friend asked him what had happened to cause the blisters.

"My wife left her hot iron on, so when the phone rang I picked the iron up by mistake."

"Yes, but what about the other ear?"

"The damned fool called back!"

A famous Viennese surgeon told his students that a surgeon needed two gifts: freedom from nausea and the power of observation.

He then dipped a finger into some nauseating fluid and licked it, requesting each of the students to do the same. They steeled themselves to it and managed it without flinching.

With a smile, the surgeon then said, "Gentlemen, I congratulate you on having passed the first test. But not, unfortunately, the second, for not one of you noticed that the finger I licked was not the one I dipped into the fluid."

AWARENESS

The priest of a fashionable parish had his ushers greet the people after Sunday service. His wife persuaded him to take on this task himself. "Wouldn't it be awful it, after some years, you were not to know the members of your own parish?" she said.

So the following Sunday the priest took up his post at the church door after service. The first one out of church was a woman in plain clothes, evidently a newcomer to the parish.

"How do you do? I am very glad to have you here with us," he said, offering her his hand.

"Thank you," said the woman, somewhat taken aback.

"I hope we will see you often at our services. We are always glad to see new faces, you know."

"Yes, sir."

"Do you live in this parish?"

The woman seemed at a loss what to say.

"If you give me your address, my wife and I will call on you some evening."

"You wouldn't have to go far, sir. I'm your cook"

A tramp stood in the office of a wealthy man asking for an alms.

The man rang for his secretary and aid, "Do you see this poor, unfortunate man here? Observe how his toes stick out of his shoes, how frayed his trousers are, how tattered his coat. I am sure the man hasn't had a shave, a shower or a decent meal in days. It breaks my heart to see people in this wretched condition—so,
GET HIM OUT OF MY SIGHT AT ONCE!"

A man with only stumps for arms and legs
was begging by the roadside.
I was so conscience stricken the first time I saw him
that I gave him an alms.
The second time I gave him less.
The third time I cold-bloodedly handed him over to the police
for begging in a public place
and making a nuisance of himself.

The Guru meditating in his Himalayan cave opened his eyes to discover an unexpected visitor sitting there before him—the abbot of a well-known monastery.

"What is it you seek?" asked the Guru.

The abbot recounted a tale of woe. At one time his monastery had been famous throughout the western world. Its cells were filled with young aspirants and its church resounded to the chant of its monks. But hard times had come on the monastery. People no longer flocked there to nourish their spirit, the stream of young aspirants had dried up, the church was silent. There was only a handful of monks left and these went about their duties with heavy hearts.

Now this is what the abbot wanted to know: "Is it because of some sin of ours that the monastery has been reduced to this state?"

"Yes," said the Guru, "a sin of ignorance."

"And what sin might that be?"

"One of your members is the Messiah in disguise and you are ignorant of this." Having said that the Guru closed his eyes and returned to his meditation.

Throughout the arduous journey back to his monastery the abbot's heart beat fast at the thought that the Messiah—but the Messiah himself—had returned to earth and was right there in the monastery. How is it he had failed to recognize him? And who could it be? Brother Cook?

Brother Sacristan? Brother Treasurer? Brother Prior? No, not he; he had too many defects, alas. But then the Guru had said he was in disguise. Could those defects be one of his disguises? Come to think of it, everyone in the monastery had defects. And one of them had to be the Messiah!

Back in the monastery he assembled the monks and told them what he had discovered. They looked at one another in disbelief. The Messiah? Here? Incredible! But he was supposed to be here in disguise. So, maybe. What if it were so-and-so? Or the other one over there? Or....

One thing was certain: If the Messiah was there in disguise it was not likely that they would recognize him. So they took to treating everyone with respect and consideration. "You never know," they said to themselves when they dealt with one another, "maybe this is the one."

The result of this was that the atmosphere in the monastery became vibrant with joy. Soon dozens of aspirants were seeking admission to the Order—and once again the Church re-echoed with the holy and joyful chant of monks who were aglow with the spirit of Love.

Of what use is it to have eyes
if the heart is blind?

A prisoner lived in solitary confinement for years. He saw and spoke to no one and his meals were served through an opening in the wall.

One day an ant came into his cell. The man contemplated it in fascination as it crawled around the room. He held it in the palm of his hand the better to observe it, gave it a grain or two, and kept it under his tin cup at night.

One day it suddenly struck him that it had taken him ten long years of solitary confinement to open his eyes to the loveliness of an ant.

When a friend visited the Spanish painter El Greco at his home on a lovely spring afternoon he found him sitting in his room, the curtains tightly drawn.

"Come out into the sunshine," said the friend.

"Not now," El Greco replied. "It would disturb the light that is shining within me."

The old rabbi had become blind and could neither read nor look at the faces of those who came to visit him.

A faith healer said to him, "Entrust yourself to my care and I will heal your blindness."

"There will be no need for that," replied the rabbi. "I can see everything that I need to."

Not everyone whose eyes are closed is asleep.
And not everyone with open eyes can see.

RELIGION

Weary traveller: "Why in the name of heaven did they build the railway station three kilometres away from the village?"

Helpful porter: "They must have thought it would be a good idea to have it near the trains, sir."

An ultra-modern station
three kilometres away from the track
is as much of an absurdity
as a much frequented temple
three centimetres away from life.

The Kamakura Buddha was lodged in a temple until one day a mighty storm brought the temple down. Then for many years the massive status stood exposed to sun and rain and wind and the changes of the weather.

When a priest began to raise funds to rebuild the temple, the statue appeared to him in a dream and said, "That temple was a prison, not a home. Leave me exposed to the ravages of life. That's where I belong."

Dov Ber was an uncommon man. When people came into his presence they trembled. He was a Talmudic scholar of repute, inflexible, uncompromising in his doctrine. And he never laughed. He believed firmly in self-inflicted pain and was known to fast for days on end Dov Ber's austerities finally got the better of him. He fell seriously ill and there was nothing the doctors could do to cure him. As a final resort someone made a suggestion: "Why not seek the help of the Baal Shem Tov?"

Dov Ber agreed even though at first he resisted the idea because he strongly disapproved of Baal Shem whom he considered to be something of a heretic. Also while Dov Ber believed that life was only made meaningful by suffering and tribulation, Baal Shem sought to alleviate pain and openly preached that it was the spirit of rejoicing that gave meaning to life.

It was past midnight when Baal Shem answered the summons and drove up dressed in a coat of wool and a cap of the finest fur. He walked into the sick man's room and handed him the Book of Splendour which Dov Ber opened and began to read aloud.

He had hardly read for a minute when, so the story goes, Baal Shem interrupted. "Something is missing," he said. "Something is lacking to your faith."

"And what is that?" the sick man asked.

"Soul," said the Baal Shem Tov.

On a cold winter night wandering ascetic asked for shelter in a temple. The poor man stood shivering there in the falling snow so the temple priest, reluctant though he was to let the man in, said, "Very well, you can stay but only for the night. This is a temple, not a hospice. In the morning you will have to go."

At dead of night the priest heard a strange crackling sound. He rushed to the temple and saw an incredible sight. There was the stranger warming himself at a fire he had lit in the temple. A wooden Buddha was missing. The priest asked, "Where is the statue?"

The wanderer pointed to the fire, then said. "I thought this cold would kill me."

The priest shouted, "Are you out of your mind? ?Do you know what you have done? That was a Buddha statue. You have burnt the Buddha!"

The fire was slowly dying out. The ascetic gazed into it and began to poke it with his stick.

"What are you doing now?" the priest yelled.

"I am searching for the bones of the Buddha whom you say I burnt."

The priest later reported the incident to a Zen Master who said. "You must be a bad priest because you valued a dead Buddha over a live man.

Tetsugen, a student of Zen, resolved on a mighty undertaking: the printing of seven thousand copies of the sutras which till then were available only in Chinese.

He travelled the length and breadth of Japan to collect funds for this project. Some wealthy people offered him as much as a hundred pieces of gold but mostly he received small coins from peasants. Tetsugen expressed equal gratitude to each donor regardless of the sum of money given.

After ten long years of travel he finally collected the funds necessary for the task. Just then the river Uji overflowed and thousands were left without food and shelter. Tetsugen spent all the money he ad collected for his cherished project on these poor people.

Then he began the work of raising funds again. Again it was several years before he got the money he needed. Then an epidemic spread all over the country, so Tetsugen gave away all he had collected to help the suffering.

Once again he set out on his travel and, twenty years later, his dream of having the scriptures in the Japanese language finally came true.

The printing block that produced this first edition of the sutras is on display at the Obaku Monastery in Kyoto. The Japanese tell their children that Tetsugen got out three editions of the sutras in all; and that the first two are invisible and far superior to the third.

Two brothers, one a bachelor, the other married, owned a farm whose fertile soil yielded an abundance of grain. Half the grain went to one brother and half to the other.

All went well at first. Then, every now and then, the married man began to wake with a start from his sleep at night and think: "This isn't fair. My brother isn't married and he gets half the produce of the farm. Here I am with a wife and five kids, so I have all the security I need for my old age. But who will care for my poor brother when he gets old? He needs to save much more for the future than he does at present. So his need is obviously greater than mine."

With that he would get out of bed, steal over to his brother's place and pour a sackful of grain into his brother's granary.

The bachelor too began to get these nightly attacks. Every once in a while he would wake from his sleep and say to himself: "This simply isn't fair. My brother has a wife and five kids and he gets half the produce of the land. Now I have no one except myself to support. So is it just that my poor brother, whose need is obviously greater than mine, should receive exactly as much as I do?" Then he would get out of bed and pour a sackful of grain into his brother's granary.

One day they got out of bed at the same time and ran into each other, each with a sack of grain on his back!

Many years later, after their death, the story leaked out. So when the townsfolk wanted to build a temple they chose the spot at which the two brothers met for they could not think of any place in the town that was holier than that one.

The important religious distinction
is not between those who worship
and those who do not worship
but between those who love
and those who don't.

A wealthy farmer burst into his home one day and cried out in an anguished voice, "Rebecca, there is a terrible story in town—the Messiah is here!"

"What's so terrible in that?" asked his wife. "I think it's great. What are you so upset about?"

"What am I so upset about?" the man exclaimed. "After all these years of sweat and toil we have finally found prosperity. We have a thousand head of cattle, our barns are full of grain and our trees laden with fruit. Now we will have to give it all away and follow him."

"Calm down," said his wife consolingly. "The Lord our God is good. He knows how much we Jews have always had to suffer. We had a Pharaoh, a Haman, a Hitler—always somebody. But our dear God found a way to deal with them all, didn't He? Just have faith, my dear husband. He will find a way to deal with the Messiah too."

Goldstein, aged ninety-two, had lived through pogroms in Poland, concentration camps in Germany and dozens of other persecutions against the Jews.

"Oh, Lord!" he said, "Isn't it true that we are your chosen people?"

A heavenly voice replied. "Yes, Goldstein, the Jews are my chosen people."

"Well, then, isn't it time you chose somebody else?"

RELIGION

An atheist fell off a cliff. As he tumbled downward he caught hold of the branch of a small tree. There he hung between heaven above and the rocks a thousand feet below, knowing he wasn't going to be able to hold on much longer.

Then an idea came to him "God!" he shouted with all his might.

Silence! No one responded.

"God!" he shouted again. "If you exist, save me and I promise I shall believe in you and teach others to believe."

Silence again! Then he almost let go of the branch in shock as he heard a mighty Voice booming across the canyon. "That's what they all say when they are in trouble."

"No, God, no!" he shouted out, more hopeful now. "I am not like the others. Why, I have already begun to believe, don't you see, having heard your Voice for myself. Now all you have to do is save me and I shall proclaim your name to the ends of the earth."

"Very well," said the Voice. "I shall save you. Let go of that branch."

"Let go of the branch?" yelled the distraught man. "Do you think I'm crazy?"

It is said that when Moses threw his wand into the Red Sea the expected miracle did not take place. It was only when the first man threw himself into the sea that the waves receded and the water divided itself to offer a dry passage to the Jews.

Mulla Nasruddin's house was on fire, so he ran up to his roof for safety. There he was, precariously perched on the rood, when his friends gathered in the street below holding a stretched out blanket to him and shouting, "Jump, Mullah, Jump!"

"Oh no, I won't," said the Mullah. "I know you fellows. If I jump, you'll pull the blanket away just to make a fool of me!"

"Don't be silly, Mullah. This isn't a joke. This is serious Jump!"

"No," said Nasruddin. "I don't trust any of you. Lay that blanket on the ground and I'll jump."

The old miser was overheard at his prayers: "If the Almighty, may His holy name be blessed forever, would give me a hundred thousand dollars, I would give ten thousand to the poor. I promise I would. And if the Almighty, may He be glorified forever, were not to trust me, let Him deduct the ten thousand in advance and just send me the balance."

Pilot to passengers in midflight: "I regret to inform you we are in terrible trouble. Only God can save us now."

A passenger turned to a priest to ask what the pilot had said and got this reply: "He says there's no hope!"

A Sufi saint, on pilgrimage to Mecca, was delighted to see that there were barely any pilgrims at the holy shrine when he got there, so he was able to perform his devotions at leisure.

Having completed the prescribed religious practices, he knelt down and touched his fore-head to the ground and said, "Allah! I have only one desire in life. Give me the grace of never offending you again."

When the All-Merciful heard this he laughed aloud and said, "That's what they all ask for. But if I granted everyone this grace, tell me, whom would I forgive?"

When the sinner was asked about the fearless way he walked into the temple, he replied: "There is no single person that sky does not cover; there is no single person that earth does not sustain—and God, is He not earth and sky to everyone?"

A priest ordered his deacon to assemble ten men to chant prayers for the recovery of a sick man.

When they had all come in, someone whispered into the ear of the priest, "There are some notorious thieves among those men."

"All the better," said the priest. "When the Gates of Mercy are shut, these are the experts who will open them."

A traveller was walking along the road one day when a man on horseback rushed by. There was an evil look in his eyes and blood on his hands.

Minutes later a crowd of riders drew up and wanted to know if the traveller had seen someone with blood on his hands go by. They were in hot pursuit of him.

"Who is he?" the traveller asked.

"An evil-doer," said the leader of the crowd.

"And you pursue him in order to bring him to justice?"

"No," said the leader, "we pursue him in order to show him the way."

Reconciliation alone will save the world,
not justice
which is generally another word for revenge.

The poet Awhadi of Kerman was sitting on his porch one night, bent over a vessel. The Sufi Shams-e-Tabrizi happened to pass by. "What are you doing?" he asked the poet.

"Contemplating the moon in a bowl of water." was the reply.

"Unless you have broken your neck, why don't you look directly at the moon in the sky?"

Words are inadequate reflections of reality. A man thought he knew what the Taj Mahal was because he was shown a piece of marble and told that the Taj was just a collection of pieces like that. Another one was convinced that, because he had seen Niagara water in a bucket, he knew what the Falls were like.

"What a pretty baby you have there!"

"This is nothing! You should see his photographs!"

Words (and concepts) are indicators,
not reflections, of reality.
But, as the mystics of the East declare.
When the Sage points to the moon
all that the idiot sees is the finger!"

A drunk was staggering across a bridge one night when he ran into a friend. The two of them leaned over the bridge and began chatting for a while.

"What's that down there?" asked the drunk suddenly.

"That's the moon. "said his friend.

The drunk looked again, shook his head in disbelief and said, "Okay, okay. But how the hell did I get way up here."

We almost never see reality.
What we see is a reflection of it
in the form of words and concepts
which we then proceed to take for reality.
The world we live in
is mostly a mental construct.

People feed on words.
live by words,
would fall apart without them.

> A beggar tugged at the sleeves of a passer-by and begged
> for money to buy a cup of coffee. This was his tale: "There
> was a time, sir, when I was a wealthy businessman just
> like you. I worked hard all day long. On my desk was
> the motto: THINK CREATIVELY, ACT DECISIVELY, LIVE
> DANGEROUSLY. That's the motto I lived by—and money
> just kept pouring in. And then… and then… (the beggar's
> frame shook with sobs)"… the cleaning woman threw my
> motto out with the trash."

When you sweep out the temple courtyard
don't stop to read the old newspapers.
When you are cleaning out your heart
don't stop to flirt with words.

RELIGION

There was once a man who was very stupid. Each morning when he woke he had such a hard time finding his clothes that he almost feared to go to bed when he thought of the trouble he would have on walking.

One night he got himself a pencil and pad and jotted down the exact name and location of each item of clothing as he undressed. Next morning he pulled out his pad and read, "pants'—there they were. He stepped into them. "Shirt"—there it was. He pulled it over his head. "Hat"—there it was. He slapped it on his head.

He was very pleased about all this till a horrible thought struck him. "And I—where am I?" He had forgotten to jot that down. So he searched and searched but in vain. He could not find himself.

What about those who say.
"I am reading this book
to find out who I am?"

One of the most renowned sages in ancient India was
Svetaketu. This is how he came by his wisdom: When
he was no more than seven years of age he was sent by
his father to study the Vedas. By dint of application and
intelligence the lad outshone all his fellow students till in
time he was considered the greatest living expert on the
Scriptures—and this when he was barely past his youth.

On his return home his father wished to test the ability of
his son. This is the question he put him: "Have you learned
that by learning which there is no need to learn anything
else? Have you discovered that by discovering which all
suffering ceases? Have you mastered that which cannot be
taught?"

"No," said Svetaketu.

"Then," said his father, "what you have learnt in all these
years in worthless, my son."

So impressed was Svetaketu by the truth of his father's
words that he set off to discover through silence the
wisdom which cannot be expressed in words.

*When the pond dries up and the fish are lying on the parched
earth, to moisten them with one's breath or damp them with spittle
is no substitute for flinging them back into the lake. Don't enliven
people with doctrines; throw them back into Reality. For the secret
of life is to be found in life itself—not in doctrines about it.*

RELIGION

A seeker asked the Sufi Jalaluddin Rumi if the Koran was a good book to read.

He replied, "You should rather ask yourself if you are in a state to profit from it."

A Christian mystic used to say of the Bible, "However useful a menu, it is not good for eating."

Child in geography class: "The benefit of longitude and latitude is that when you are drowning you can call out what longitude and latitude you are in and they will find you."

Because there is a word for wisdom
People imagine they know what it is.
But no one becomes an astronomer
from understanding the meaning
of the word "astronomy."

Just because, by blowing on the thermometer,
you got it to register higher,
you did not warm the room.

Every day in the corner of a library in Japan an old monk was to be found sitting in peaceful meditation.

"I never see you read the sutras," said the librarian.

"I never learnt to read," replied the monk.

"That's a disgrace. A monk like you ought to be able to read. Shall I teach you?"

"Yes. Tell me," said the monk pointing to himself, "What is the meaning of this character?"

Why light a torch
when the sun shines in the heavens?
Why water the ground
When the rain pours down in torrents?

RELIGION

A Guru promised a scholar a revelation of greater consequence than anything contained in the scriptures.

When the scholar eagerly asked for it, the Guru said, "Go out into the rain and raise your head and arms heavenward. That will bring you the first revelation."

The next day the scholar came to report: "I followed your advice and water flowed down my neck—And I felt like a perfect fool."

"Well," said the Guru, "For the first day that's quite a revelation, isn't it?"

The poet Kabir says:

What good is it if the scholar pores over words and points of this and that but his chest is not soaked dark with love?

What good is it if the ascetic clothes himself in saffron robes but is colourless within?

What good is it if you scrub your ethical behaviour till it shines, but there is no music inside?

Disciple:	What's the difference between knowledge and enlightenment?
Master:	When you have knowledge you use a torch to show the way. When you are enlightened you become a torch.

A Parachutist jumped out of a plane on a windy day and was blown a hundred miles off course by a powerful gale. Then his parachute caught on a tree, so he hung there for hours in the middle of nowhere, shouting for help.

Finally someone passed by. "How did you get up there on that tree?" he asked.

The parachutist told him. Then asked, "Where am I?"

"On a tree," was the reply.

"Hey! You must be a cleric!"

The stranger was stunned, "Yes I am. How did you know?"

"Because what you said is certainly true and just as certainly useless."

A group was enjoying the music at a Chinese restaurant. Suddenly a soloist struck up a vaguely familiar tune; everyone recognized the melody but no one could remember its name. So they beckoned to the splendidly-clad waiter and asked him to find out what the musician was playing. The waiter waddled across the floor, then returned with a look of triumph on his face and declared in a loud whisper, "Violin!"

The scholar's contribution to spirituality!

RELIGION

The play was in progress at the village theatre when the curtain was suddenly lowered and the manager stepped before the audience.

"Ladies and gentlemen," he said, "it distresses me deeply to have to announce that the leading actor, our great and beloved mayor himself, has just had a fatal heart attack in his dressing room. We are therefore forced to stop the play."

On hearing this announcement a huge middle-aged woman in the front row stood up and shouted agitatedly: "Quick! Give him chicken broth!"

"Madam," said the manager, "the heart attack was fatal. The man is dead!"

"So give it to him at once!"

The manager was desperate. "Madam," he pleaded, "What good will chicken broth do to a dead man?"

"What harm will it do?" she shouted.

Chicken broth does for the dead
what religion does for the unconscious
whose number, alas, is legion.

A Master was surprised to hear shouting and altercation going on in his courtyard. When he was told that one of his disciples was at the centre of it, he had the man sent for and asked what the cause of the din was.

"There is a delegation of scholars that has come to visit you. I told them you do not waste your time on men whose heads are stuffed with books and thought but devoid of wisdom. These are the people who, in their conceit, create dogmas and divisions among people everywhere."

The Master smiled. "How true, how true," he murmured. "But tell me, is not your conceit in claiming to be different from the scholars the cause of this present conflict and division?"

A Hindu Sage was having the Life of Jesus read to him.

When he learned how Jesus was rejected by his people in Nazareth, he exclaimed, "A rabbi whose congregation does not want to drive him out of town isn't a rabbi."

And when he heard how it was the priests who put Jesus to death, he said with a sigh, "It is hard for Satan to mislead the whole world, so he appoints prominent ecclesiastics in different parts of the globe."

The lament of a bishop: "Wherever Jesus went there was a revolution; wherever I go people serve tea!"

When a million people follow you ask yourself where you have gone wrong.

A Jewish author explains that Jews are not proselytizers. Rabbis are required to make three separate efforts to discourage prospective converts!

Spirituality is for the elite. It will not compromise to become acceptable so it will not consort with the masses who want syrup, not medicine. Once, when large crowds were following Jesus, this is what he said to them:

"Which of you would think of building a tower without first sitting down and estimating the cost to see if he can afford to finish it? Or what king will march to battle against another king without first sitting down to consider if with ten thousand soldiers he will be able to do battle with an enemy who comes to meet him with twenty thousand? If he cannot, then, long before the enemy is near, he sends emissaries and asks for terms. So also none of you can be a disciple of mine without the readiness to renounce all possessions."

People do not want truth.
They want reassurance.

Said a preacher to a friend, "We have just had the greatest revival our church has experienced in many years."

"How many did you add to your church membership?"

"None. We lost five hundred."

Jesus would have applauded!

Experience shows, alas, that our religious convictions bear as much relation to our personal holiness as a man's dinner jacket to his digestion.

An ancient philosopher, dead for many centuries, was told that his teachings were being misrepresented by his representatives. Being a compassionate and truthloving individual, he managed, after much effort, to get the grace to come back to earth for a few days.

It took him several days to convince his successors of his identity. Once that was established, they promptly lost all interest in what he had to say and begged him to disclose to them the secret for coming back to life from the grave.

It was only after considerable exertion that he finally convinced them that there was no way he could impart this secret to them and that it was infinitely more important for the good of humanity that they restore his teaching to its original purity.

A futile task! What they said to him was, "Don't you see that what is important is not what you taught but our interpretation of what you taught? After all, you are only a bird of passage whereas we reside here permanently."

When Buddha dies, the schools are born.

All the philosophers, divines and doctors of the law were assembled in court for the trial of Mullah Nasruddin. The accusation was a serious one; he had been going from town to town saying, "Your so-called religious leaders are ignorant and confused." So he was charged with heresy, the penalty for which was death.

"You may speak first," said the Caliph.

The Mullah was perfectly self-possessed. "Have paper and pens brought in," he said, "and give them to the ten wisest men in this august assembly."

To Nasruddin's amusement, a great squabble broke out among the holy men as to who was the wisest among them. When the contention died down and each of the chosen ten was equipped with paper and pen, the Mullah said, "Have each of them write down the answer to the following question: WHAT IS MATTER MADE OF?"

The answers were written down and handed to the Caliph who read them out. One said, "It is made of nothing." Another said, "Molecules." Yet another, "Energy." Others, "Light," "I do not know," "Metaphysical Being" and so on.

Said Nasruddin to the Caliph, "When they come to an agreement on what matter is, they will be fit to judge questions of the spirit. Is it not strange that they cannot agree on something that they themselves are made of, yet they are unanimous in their verdict that I am a heretic?"

It is not the diversity of our dogmas
but our dogmatism
that does the damage.
Thus, if each of us did what we are firmly persuaded
is the will of God
the result would be utter chaos.
The spiritual person known uncertainty—
a state of mind unknown to the religious fanatic:

One night a fisherman stole into the grounds of a rich man and cast his net into a lake full of fish. The owner heard him and set his guards upon him.

When he saw the crowd searching for him everywhere with lighted torches, the fisherman hastily smeared his body with ashes and sat under a tree, as is the custom with holy men in India.

The owner and his guards could find no poacher, though they searched for a long time. All they found was a holy man covered with ashes sitting under a tree absorbed in meditation.

The next day word spread everywhere that a great sage had designed to take up residence in the grounds of the rich man. People gathered with flowers and fruits and food and even a lot of money to pay obeisance to him for it is piously believed that gifts, when made to a holy man, bring God's blessing upon the giver.

The fisherman turned sage was astounded at his good fortune. "It is easier to make a living on the faith of these people than by the toil of my hands," he said to himself. So he continued to meditate and never went back to work again.

A king dreamt that he saw a king in paradise and a priest in hell. He wondered how this could be, then he heard a Voice say, "The king is in paradise because he respected priests. The priest is in hell because he compromised with kings."

When Sister asked the children in her class what they wanted to be when they grew up little Tommy said he wanted to be a pilot. Elsie said she wanted to be a doctor, Bobby to Sister's great joy, said he wanted to become a priest. Then Mary stood up and declared she wanted to be a prostitute.

"What was that again, Mary?"

"When I grow up," said Mary with the air of someone who knew exactly what she wanted, "I shall become a prostitute."

Sister was startled beyond words. Mary was immediately segregated from the rest of the children and taken to the Parish Priest.

Father was given the facts in broad outline but he wanted to check them out with the culprit. "Tell me what happened in your own words, Mary."

"Well," said Mary, somewhat taken aback by all this fuss, "Sister asked me what I wanted to become when I grew up and I said I wanted to become a prostitute."

"Did you say prostitute?" asked Father, double-checking.

"Yes."

"Heavens! What a relief! We all thought you said you were going to become a Protestant!"

Rabbi Abraham had lived had lived an exemplary life. And when his time arrived, he left this world surrounded by the blessings off his congregation who had come to regard him as a saint and as the principal cause of all the blessings they had received from God.

It was no different at the other end, for the angels came forward to welcome him with shouts of praise. Throughout the festivities the Rabbi seemed withdrawn and distressed. He kept his head in his hands and refused to be comforted. He was finally taken before the Judgement Seat where he felt himself enveloped by a Loving Kindness that was infinite and he heard a Voice of infinite tenderness say to him, "What is it that distresses you, my son?"

"Most Holy One," replied the Rabbi, "I am unworthy of all the honours that are bestowed on me here. Even though I was considered to be an example to the people, there must have been something wrong with my life, for my only son, in spite of my example and my teaching, abandoned our faith and became a Christian."

"Let that not disturb you, my son. I understand exactly how you feel, for I have a son who did the same thing!"

In Belfast, Ireland, a Catholic priest, a Protestant minister and a Jewish rabbi were engaged in a heated theological discussion. Suddenly an Angel appeared in their midst and said to them, "God sends you his blessings. Make one wish for Peace and your wish will be fulfilled by the Almighty."

The minister said, "Let every Catholic disappear from our lovely island. Then peace will reign supreme."

The priest said, "Let there not be a single Protestant left on our sacred Irish soil. That will bring peace to this island."

"And what about you, Rabbi?" said the Angel. "Do you have no wish of your own?"

"No," said the rabbi. "Just attend to the wishes of these two gentlemen and I shall be well pleased."

Little boy: "Are you a Presbyterian?"
Little girl: "No. We belong to a different abomination."

A hunter sent his dog after something that moved behind the trees. It chased out a fox and coralled it into a position where the hunter could shoot it.

The dying fox said to the hound, "Were you never told that the fox is brother to the dog?"

"I was, indeed," said the dog. "But that's for idealists and fools. For the practical-minded, brotherhood is created by identity of interests."

Said the Christian to the Buddhist: "We could be brothers, really. But that's for idealists and fools. For the practical-minded, brotherhood lies in identity of beliefs.

Most people, alas, have enough religion to hate but not enough to love.

In his autobiography, Mahatma Gandhi tells how in his student days in South Africa he became deeply interested in the Bible, especially the Sermon on the Mount.

He become convinced that Christianity was the answer to the caste system that had plagued India for centuries, and he seriously considered becoming a Christian.

One day he went to a church to attend Mass and get instructions. He was stopped at the entrance and gently told that if he desired to attend Mass he was welcome to do so in a church reserved for blacks.

He left and never returned.

A public sinner was excommunicated and forbidden entry to the church.

He took his woes to God. "They won't let me in, Lord, because I am a sinner."

"What are you complaining about?" said God. "They won't let me in either!"

A church or synagogue needs to raise money if it is to survive. Now there was once a Jewish synagogue where they did not pass the collection plate around as they do in Christian Churches. Their way of raising money was to sell tickets for reserved seats on solemn Holy Days for that was when the congregation was the largest and the people most generous.

On one such Holy Day a kid came to the synagogue in search of his father but the ushers wouldn't let him in because he did not have a ticket.

"Look," said the youngster, "this is a very important matter."

"That's what they all say," the usher replied, unmoved.

The lad became desperate and began to plead. "Please sir, let me in. This is a matter of life and death. I'll only be in a minute."

The usher relented. "Well, OK if it is so important," he said, "But don't let me catch you praying!"

Organised Religion has its limitations, alas!

RELIGION

The preacher was more than ordinarily eloquent and everyone, but everyone, was moved to tears. Well, not everyone exactly, because there, in the front pew, sat a gentleman looking straight in front of him, quite unaffected by the sermon.

At the end of the service, someone said to him, "You heard the sermon, didn't you?"

"Of course, I did," said the stony gentleman.
"I am not deaf."

"What did you think of it?"

"I thought it so moving I could have cried."

"And why, may I ask, did you not cry?"

"Because," said the gentleman, "I do not belong to this parish."

According to one story, when God created the world and glorified in its goodness, Satan shared his rapture, in his own way, of course, for as he contemplated marvel after marvel, he kept exclaiming, "How good it is! Let's organize it!"

"And take all the fun out of it!"

Have you ever attempted to organize something like peace?
The moment you do,
You have power conflicts
and group wars within the organization.
The only way to have peace
is to let it grow wild.

A bishop was testing the suitability of a group of candidates for baptism.

"By what sign will others know that you are Catholics?" he asked.

There was no reply. Evidently no one had expected this question. The bishop repeated the question. Then he said it once again, this time making the Sign of the Cross to give the others a clue to the right answer.

Suddenly one of the candidates got it. "Love" he said.

The bishop was taken aback. He was about to say. "Wrong," then checked himself in the nick of time.

Someone asked for the bishop's imprimatur for a book for children that contained the parables of Jesus, a few simple illustrations and a few gospel sentences. Not a single word more.

The imprimatur was given with the customary disclaimer: "The imprimatur does not necessarily imply that the bishop agrees with the opinions expressed in this book."

More organizational pitfalls!

How spiritual organizations grow:

A Guru so impressed by the spiritual progress of his disciple that, judging he needed no further guidance, he left him on his own in a little hut on the banks of a river.

Each morning after his ablutions the disciple would hang his loin-cloth out to dry. It was his only possession! One day he was dismayed to find it torn to shreds by rats. So he had to beg for another from the villagers. When the rats nibbled holes in this one too, he got himself a kitten. He had no more trouble with the rats but now, in addition to begging for his own food, he had to beg for milk as well.

"Too much trouble begging," he thought, "and too much of a burden on the villagers. I shall keep a cow." When he got the cow, he had to beg for fodder. "Easter to till the land around my hut," he thought. But that proved troublesome too for it left him little time for meditation. So he employed labourers to till the land for him. Now overseeing the labourers became a chore, so he married a wife who would share this task with him. Before long, of course, he was one of the wealthiest men in the village.

Years later his Guru happened to drop by and was surprised to see a palatial mansion where once a hut had stood. He said to one of the servants, 'Isn't this where a disciple of mine used to live?"

Before he got a reply, the disciple himself emerged. "What's the meaning of all this, my son?" asked the Guru.

"You're not going to believe this, sir," said the man, "but there was no other way I could keep my loin-cloth!"

On a rocky seacoast where shipwrecks were frequent there was once a ramshackle little life-saving station. It was no more than a hut and there was only one boat, but the few people who manned the station were a devoted lot who kept constant watch over the sea and, with little regard for themselves and their safety, went fearlessly out in a storm if they had any evidence that there had been a shipwreck somewhere. Many lives were thus saved and the station became famous.

As the fame of the station grew, so did the desire of people in the neighbourhood to become associated with its excellent work. They generously offered their time and money so new members were enrolled, new boats bought and new crews trained. The hut too was replaced by a comfortable building which could adequately handle the needs of those who had been saved from the sea and, of course, since shipwrecks do not occur every day, it became a popular gathering place—a sort of local club. As time passed the members became so engaged in socializing that they had little interest in life-saving, though they duly sported the life-saving motto on the badges they wore. As a matter of fact, when some people were actually rescued from the sea, it was always such a nuisance because they were dirty and sick and soiled the carpeting and the furniture.

Soon the social activities of the club became so numerous and the life-saving activities so few that there was a show-down at a club meeting with some members insisting that they return to their original purpose and activity. A vote was taken and these troublemakers, who proved to be a small minority, were invited to leave the club and start another.

Which is precisely what they did—a little further down the coast, with such selflessness and daring that after a while their heroism made them famous. Whereupon their membership was enlarged, their hut was reconstructed.. and their idealism smothered. If you happen to visit that area today you will find a number of exclusive clubs dotting the shoreline. Each one of them is justifiably proud of its origin and its tradition. Shipwrecks still occur in those parts, but nobody seems to care much.

In a desert country trees were scarce and fruit was hard to come by. It was said that God wanted to make sure there was enough for everyone, so He appeared to a prophet and said, "This is my commandment to the whole people for now and for future generations: no one shall eat more than one fruit a day. Record this in the Holy Book. Anyone who transgresses this law will be considered to have sinned against God and against humanity."

The law was faithfully observed for centuries until scientists discovered a means for turning the desert into green land. The country became rich in grain and livestock. And the trees bent down with the weight of unplucked fruit. But the fruit law continued to be enforced by the civil and religious authorities of the land.'

Anyone who pointed to the sin against humanity involved in allowing fruit to rot on the ground was dubbed a blasphemer and an enemy of morality. These people, who questioned the wisdom of God's Holy word, were being guided by the proud spirit of reason, it was said, and lacked the spirit of faith and submission whereby alone the Truth can be received.

In the churches sermons were frequently delivered in which those who broke the law were shown to have come to a bad end. Never once was mention made of the equal number of those who came to a bad end even though they had faithfully kept the law or on the vast number of those who prospered even though they broke it.'

Nothing could be done to change the law because the prophet who had claimed to have received it from God was long since dead. He might have had the courage and the sense to change the law as circumstances changed for he had taken God's Word, not as something to be revered, but as something to be used for the welfare of the people.

As a result, some people openly scoffed at the law and at God and religion. Others broke it secretly and always with a sense of wrongdoing. The vast majority adhered rigorously to it and came to think of themselves as holy merely because they held on to a senseless and outdated custom they were too frightened to jettison.

RELIGION

Among the truly religious
the Law is observed.
But it is neither feared....

"What do you do for a living?" asked a lady of a young man at a cocktail party.

"I am a paratrooper."

"It must be awful to be a parachute jumper,"
said the lady.

"Well, it does have its scary moments."

"Tell me about your most terrible experience."

"Well," said the paratrooper, "I think it was the time when I came down on a lawn where there was a sign which read, KEEP OFF THE GRASS.

...nor revered...

A sergeant was asking a group of recruits why walnut was used for the butt of a rifle.

"Because it is harder than other wood," said one man.

"Wrong," said the sergeant.

"Because it is more elastic."

"Wrong again."

"Because it has a better shine."

"You boys certainly have a lot to learn. Walnut is used for the simple reason that it is laid down in the Regulations!"

...it is neither absolutized...

A railway official reported a murder on a train in the following terms: "The assassin entered the coach from the platform. Stabbed the victim savagely five times, each time inflicting a mortal blow, and left the train by the opposite door, alighting upon the railway track—thereby transgressing Railway Regulations."

A nobleman was criticized for burning down a cathedral. He said he was truly sorry but had been informed—falsely, as it turned out—that the Archbishop was inside!

In a small town a man dialled 016 for directory information. A woman's voice at the other end said, "I'm sorry, you will have to dial 015 for that."

It seemed to him, when he had dialled 015, that he was hearing the same voice at the other end. So he said, "Aren't you the lady whom I spoke to a while ago?"

"I am," said the voice. "I'm doing both jobs today."

...nor magnified out of all proportion...

Mr. Smith had killed his wife and his defence was temporary insanity. He was in the witness stand and his lawyer asked him to describe the crime in his own words.

'Your Honour," he said, "I am a quiet man of regular habits who lives at peace with all the world. Each day I wake at seven, have breakfast at seven-thirty, show up for work at nine, leave work at five come home at six, find supper on the table, eat it, read the papers, watch television, then retire for the night. Until the day in question.."

Here his breathing accelerated and a look of fury came upon him.

"Go on," said the lawyer quietly. "Tell this court what happened."

"On the day in question I woke up at seven, as usual, had my breakfast at seven-thirty, got to work at nine, left at five, got home at six and I discovered to my dismay that supper wasn't on the table. There was no sign of my wife either. So I searched through the house and found her in bed with a strange man. So I shot her."

"Describe your emotions at the time you killed her," said the lawyer, anxious to make his point.

"I was in an uncontrollable rage. I just went out of my mind. Your Honour, ladies and gentlemen of the jury," he shouted pounding the arm of his chair with his fist, "When I get home at six I absolutely demand that supper be ready on the table!"

...nor exploited.

Mullah Nasruddin found a diamond by the road-side but, according to the Law, finders became keepers only if they first announced their find in the centre of the marketplace on three separate occasions.

Now Nasruddin was too religious-minded to disregard the Law and too greedy to run the risk of parting with his find. So on three consecutive nights when he was sure that everyone was fast asleep he went to the centre of the marketplace and there announced in a soft voice, "I have found a diamond on the road that leads to the town. Anyone knowing who the owner is should contact me at once."

No one was the wiser for the Mullah's words, of course, except for one man who happened to be standing at his window on the third night and heard the Mullah mumble something. When he attempted to find out what it was, Nasruddin replied, "I am in no way obliged to tell you. But this much I shall say: Being a religious man, I went out there at night to pronounce certain words in fulfilment of the Law."

To be properly wicked,
you do not have to break the Law.
Just observe it to the letter.

Among Jews, the observance of the Sabbath, the day of the Lord, was originally a thing of joy but too many Rabbis kept issuing one injunction after another on how exactly it was to be observed, what sort of activity was allowed, until some people felt they could hardly move during the sabbath for fear that some regulation or other might be transgressed.

The Ball Shem, son of Eliezer, gave much thought to this matter. One night he had a dream. An angel took him up to heaven and showed him two thrones placed far above all others.

"For whom are these reserved?" he asked.

"For you," was the answer, "if you make use of your intelligence; and for a man whose name and address is now being written down and given to you."

He was then taken to the deepest spot in hell and shown two vacant seats. "For whom are these prepared?" he asked.

"For you," the answer came, "if you do not make use of your intelligence; and for the man whose name and address are being written down for you."

In his dream Baal Shem visited the man who was to be his companion in paradise. He found him living among Gentiles, quite ignorant of Jewish customs and, on the sabbath, he would give a banquet at which there was a lot of merrymaking and to which all his Gentile neighbours were invited. When Baal Shem asked him why he held this banquet, the man replied, "I recall that in my childhood

112

my parents taught me that the sabbath was a day for rest and for rejoicing; so on Saturdays my mother made the most succulent meals at which we sang and danced and made merry. I do the same today."

Baal Shem attempted to instruct the man in the ways of his religion for he had been born a Jew but was evidently quite ignorant of all the rabbinical prescriptions. But he was struck dumb when he realised that the man's joy in the sabbath would be marred if he was made aware of his short-comings.

Baal Shem, still in his dream, then went to the home of his companion in hell. He found the man to be a strict observer of the Law, always apprehensive lest his conduct should not be correct. The poor man spent each sabbath day in a scrupulous tension as if he were sitting on hot coals. When Baal Shem attempted to upbraid him for his slavery to the Law, the power of speech was taken from him as he realised that the man would never understand that he could do wrong by fulfilling religious injunctions.

Thanks so this revelation given him in the form of a dream, the Baal Shem Tov evolved a new system of observance whereby God is worshipped in joy that comes from the heart.

When people are joyful
they are always good;
whereas when they are good
they are seldom joyful.

113

The priest announced that Jesus Christ himself was coming to church the following Sunday. People turned up in large number to see him. Everyone expected him to preach, but he only smiled when introduced and said, "Hello," Everyone offered him hospitality for the night, especially the priest, but he refused politely. He said he would spent the night in church. How fitting, everyone thought.

He slipped away early next morning before the Church doors were opened. And, to their horror, the priest and people found their church had been vandalised. Scribbed everywhere on the walls was the single word BEWARE. No part of the church was spared: the doors and windows, the pillars and the pulpit, the altar, even the bible that rested on the lectern. BEWARE. Scratched in large letters and in small, in pencil and pen and paint of every conceivable colour. Whereever the eye rested one could see the words, "BEWARE, beware, Beware, BEWARE, beware, beware..."

Shocking, Irritating. Confusing. Fascinating. Terrifying. What were they supposed to beware of? It did not say. It just said, BEWARE. The first impulse of the people was to wipe out every trace of this defilement, this sacrilege. They were restrained from doing this only by the thought that it was Jesus himself who had done the deed.

Now that mysterious word BEWARE began to sink into the minds of the people each time they came to church. They began to beware of the scriptures, so they were able to profit from the scriptures without falling into bigotry. They began to beware of sacraments, so they were sanctified without becoming superstitious. The priest began to beware of his power over the people, so he was able to help without controlling. And everyone began to beware of religion which leads the unwary to self-righteousness. They began to beware of church law, so they became law-abiding, yet compassionate to the weak. They began to beware of prayer, so it no longer stopped them from becoming self-reliant. They even began to beware of their notions of God so they were able to recognize him outside the narrow confines of their church.

They have now inscribed the shocking word over the entrance of their church and as you drive past at night you can see it blazing above the church in multicoloured neon lights.

GRACE

A priest was sitting at his desk by the window composing a sermon on Providence when he heard something that sounded like an explosion. Soon he saw people running to and fro in a panic and discovered that a dam had burst, the river was in spate and the people were being evacuated.

The priest saw the water begin to rise in the street below. He had some difficulty suppressing his own rising sense of panic but he said to himself, "Here I am preparing a sermon about Providence and I am being given an occasion to practise what I preach. I shall not flee with the rest. I shall stay right here and trust in the providence of God to save me.

By the time the water reached his window a boat full of people came by. "Jump in, Father," they shouted. "Ah no, my children," said Father confidently. "I trust in the providence of God to save me."

Father did climb to the roof, however, and when the water got up there another boatload of people went by, urging Father to join them. Again he refused.

This time he climbed to the top of the belfry. When the water came up to his knees an officer in a motorboat was sent to rescue him. "No thank you, officer," said Father, with a calm smile. "I trust in God, you see. He will never let me down."

When Father drowned and went to heaven the first thing he did was to complain to God "I trusted you! Why did you do nothing to save me?"

"Well," said God. "I did send three boats, you know."

Two monks were on their travels. One of them practised the spirituality of acquisition, the other believed in renunciation. All day long they discussed their respective spiritualities till, towards evening they came to the bank of a river.

Now the believer in renunciation had no money with him. He said, "We cannot pay the boatman to take us across, but why bother about the body? We shall spend the night here, chanting God's praises and tomorrow we are sure to find some kind soul who will pay our passage."

The other said, "There is no village on this side of the river, no hamlet, no hut, no shelter. We shall be devoured by wild beasts or bitten by snakes or killed by the cold. On the other side of the river we shall be able to spend the night in safety and comfort. I have the money to pay the boatman."

Once they were safely on the other bank he remonstrated with his companion. "Do you see the value of keeping money? I was able to save your life and mine. What would have happened to us if I had been a man of renunciation like you?"

The other replied, "It was your renunciation that brought us across to safety, for you did part with your money to pay the boatman, didn't you? Moreover, having no money in my pocket, your pocket became mine. I have observed that I never suffer; I am always provided for."

At a party in Japan a visitor was introduced to a popular Japanese drink. After his first drink he noticed the furniture in the room moving around.

"This is a very powerful drink," he said to his host.

"Not particularly," the host replied. "This happens to be an earthquake."

An elephant broke loose from the herd and charged across a little wooden structure that stretched across a ravine.

The worn-out bridge shivered and groaned, barely able to support the elephant's weight.

Once it had gone safely to the other side, a flea that had lodged itself in the elephant's ear exclaimed in mighty satisfaction, "Boy, did we shake that bridge!"

An old woman observed how, with scientific precision, her rooster would begin to crow just before the sun rose each day. She therefore came to the conclusion that the crowing of her rooster caused the sun to rise.

So when her rooster suddenly died she hastened to replace it with another lest the sun fail to rise the following morning.

One day she fell out with her neighbours and threatened to move out of the village with her sister several miles away.

When her rooster started to crow next day and, a little later, the sun began to rise serenely above the horizon, she was confirmed in what she had known all along: the sun was now rising here and her village was in darkness Well, they had asked for it!

It did cause her to wonder, though, that her former neighbours never came to beg her to return to the village with her rooster. She just put it down to their stubbornness and stupidity.

"So this was your first flight. Were you scared?"

"Well, to tell you the truth. I didn't dare put my full weight down on the seat."

122

A disciple came riding on his camel to the tent of his Sufi Master. He dismounted and walked right into the tent, bowed low and said, "So great is my trust in God that I have left my camel outside untied, convinced that God protects the interests of those who love him."

"Go tie your camel, you fool!" said the Master. God cannot be bothered doing for you what you are perfectly capable of doing for yourself."

✳ ✳ ✳

Goldberg had the loveliest garden in town and each time the Rabbi passed by he would call out to Goldberg, "Your garden is a thing of beauty. The Lord and you are partners!"

"Thank you, Rabbi," Goldberg would respond with a bow.

This went on for days and weeks and months. At least twice a day the Rabbi, on his way to and from the synagogue would call out, "The Lord and you are partners!" until Goldberg began to be annoyed at what the Rabbi evidently meant as a compliment.

So the next time the Rabbi said, "The Lord and you are partners," Goldberg replied, "That may be true. But you should have seen this garden when the Lord had it all on his own!"

In his Narrative of the Saints, Attar tells of the great sufi Habib Ajami who went to bathe in the river one day leaving his coat lying unattended on the bank. Now Hasan of Basra happened to pass by, saw the coat and, thinking that in had been left there through someone's carelessness, decided to stand guard over it till the owner showed up.

When Habib came looking for his coat, Hasan said, "In whose care did you leave this coat of yours when you went to bathe in the river? It could have been stolen!"

Habib replied, "I left it in the care of Him who gave you the task of standing guard over it!"

A man was lost in a desert. Later, when describing his ordeal to his friends, he told how, in sheer despair, he had knelt down and cried out to God to help him.

"And did God answer your prayer?" he was asked.

"Oh no! Before He could, an explorer appeared and showed me the way."

A group of expectant fathers sat nervously in the hall. A nurse beckoned to one of them and said, "Congratulations, you have a son!"

Another man dropped his magazine, jumped up and cried, "Hey, what's the idea? I got here two hours before he did!"

Some things, alas, resist organization!

The President of the largest Banking Corporation in the world was in hospital. One of the Vice-Presidents came to visit him with this message: "I bring you the good wishes of our Board of Directors, that you should be restored to health and live to be a hundred years. That's an official resolution passed by a majority of 15 to 6 with 2 abstentions."

Are we ever likely to stop our efforts
to burn fire,
wet water
and add colour to the rose?

A family of refugees was very favourably impressed with America—especially the six-year-old daughter who rapidly adopted the view that everything American was not only the best but also perfect.

One day a neighbour told her she was going to have a baby, so little Mary marched home and demanded to know why she couldn't have a little baby too. Her mother decided to introduce her to the facts of life right there and, among other things, explained that it took about nine months for a baby to arrive.

"Nine months!" exclaimed Mary indignantly. "But mother, aren't you forgetting that this is America?"

"Mummy, I want a baby brother."

"But you've just got one."

"I want another."

"Well, you can't have one so soon. It takes time to produce a baby brother."

"Why don't you do what Daddy does at the factory?"

"What's that?"

"Put more men on the job."

A woman dreamt she walked into a brand new shop in the marketplace and, to her surprise, found God behind the counter.

"What do you sell here?" she asked

"Everything your heart desires," said God.

Hardly daring to believe that she was hearing, the woman decided to ask for the best things a human being could wish for. "I want peace of mind and love and happiness and wisdom and freedom from fear," she said. Then as an after thought, she added, "Not just for me. For everyone on earth."

God smiled, "I think you've got me wrong, my dear," He said. "We don't sell fruits here. Only seeds."

A devout religious man fell on hard times. So he took to praying in the following fashion: "Lord, remember all the years I served you as best I could, asking for nothing in return. Now that I am old and bankrupt I am going to ask you for a favour for the first time in my life and I am sure you will not say No: allow me to win the lottery."

Days passed. Then weeks and months. But nothing happened. Finally, almost driven to despair, he cried out one night, "Why don't you give me a break, God?"

He suddenly heard the voice of God replying, "Give me a break yourself! Why don't you buy a lottery ticket?"

A young composer once came to consult Mozart on how to develop his talent.

'I would advise you to start with simple thing," Mozart said. "Songs, for example."

"But you were composing symphonies when you were a child!" the man protested.

"True enough. But then I didn't have to go to anyone for advice on how to develop my talent."

A man in his eighties was once asked the secret of his enormous stamina.

"Well," he answered, "I don't drink, I don't smoke. And I swim a mile a day."

"But I had an uncle who did exactly that, and he died at the age of sixty."

"Ah, the trouble with your uncle was he didn't do it long enough."

One Sunday morning after church God and St Peter went to play golf. God teed off. He gave a mighty swipe and sliced the ball off into the rough beside the fairway.

Just as the ball was about to hit the ground, a rabbit darted out of a bush, picked it up in his mouth and ran with it down the fairway. Suddenly an eagle swooped down, picked the rabbit up in its claws and flew it over the green. A man with a rifle took aim and shot the eagle in midflight. The eagle let go of the rabbit. The rabbit fell onto the green and the ball rolled out of its mouth into the hole.

St Peter turned to God in annoyance and said, "Come on now! Do you want to play golf or do you want to fool around?"

And how about you? Do you want to understand and play the game of life or fool around with miracles?

Some things are best left as they are:

An enthusiastic young man who had just graduated as a plumber was taken to see Niagara Falls. He studied it for a minute, then said, "I think I can fix this."

THE SAINTS

Some are born holy,
others achieve holiness,
others yet have holiness thrust on them.

An oil well caught fire and the company called in the experts to put out the blaze. But so intense was the heat that the fire-fighters could not get within a thousand feet of the rig. The management, in desperation, called the local volunteer Fire Department to help in any way they could. Half an hour later a decrepit looking fire truck rolled down the road and came to an abrupt stop just fifty feet away from the devouring flames. The men jumped out of the truck, sprayed one another, then went on to put the fire out.

The management, in gratitude, held a ceremony some days later at which the courage of the local fire-men was commended, their dedication to duty extolled—and an enormous cheque was presented to the chief of the fire department. When asked by reporters what he planned to do with the cheque, the chief replied, "Well, the first thing I'm going to do is take that fire truck to a garage and have the damned brakes repaired!"

For others, alas, holiness is no more than a ritual.

* * *

Lady Pumphampton's gentleman friend had come to tea, so she gave her maid a large tip and said, "Here, take this. When you hear me scream for help, you may leave for the day."

133

𝕿here once lived a man so godly that even the angels rejoiced at the sight of him. But, in spite of his great holiness, he had no notion that he was holy. He just went about his humdrum tasks diffusing goodness the way flowers unselfconsciously diffuse their fragrance and street-lamps their glow.

His holiness lay in this that the forgot each person's past and looked at them as they were now, and he looked beyond each person's appearance to the very centre of their being where they were innocent and blameless and too ignorant to know what they were doing. Thus he loved and forgave everyone he met—and he saw nothing extraordinary in this for it was the result of his way of looking at people.

One day an angel said to him. "I have been sent to you by God. Ask for anything you wish and it will be given to you. Would you wish to have the gift of healing?" "No," said the man. "I'd rather God did the healing himself."

"Would you want to bring sinners back to the path of righteousness?" "No," he said. "it is not for me to touch human hearts. That is the work of angels." "Would you like to be such a model of virtue that people will be drawn to imitate you?" "No," said the saint "for that would make me the centre of attention."

"What then do you wish for?" asked the angel. "The grace of God," was the man's reply. "Having that, I have all I desire." "No, you must ask for some miracle," said the angel, "or one will be forced on you." "Well, then I shall ask for this: let good be done through me without my being aware of it."

So it was decreed that the holy man's shadow would be endowed with healing properties whenever it fell behind him. So everywhere his shadow fell—provided he had his back to it—the sick were healed, the land became fertile, fountains sprang to life and colour returned to the faces of those who were weighed down by life's sorrow.

But the saint knew nothing of this because the attention of people was so centred on the shadow that they forgot about the man and so his wish that good be done through him and he forgotten was abundantly fulfilled.

Holiness, like greatness, is unselfconscious.

For thirty-five years Paul Cezanne lived in obscurity producing masterpieces that he gave away to unsuspecting neighbours. So great was his love for his work that he never gave a thought to achieving recognition nor did he suspect that some day he would be looked upon as the father of modern painting.

He owes his fame to a Paris dealer who chanced upon some of his paintings, put some of them together and presented the world of art with the first Cezanne exhibition. The world was astonished to discover the presence of a master.

The master was just as astonished. He arrived at the art gallery leaning on the arm of his son and could not contain his amazement when he saw his paintings on display. Turning to his son he said, "Look, they have framed them!"

Buddha's disciple Subhuti suddenly discovered the richness and fecundity of emptiness: the realisation that everything is impermanent, unsatisfactory and empty of self. In this mood of divine of emptiness he sat in bliss under a tree when suddenly flowers began to fall all around him.

And the gods whispered, "We are enraptured by your sublime teachings on emptiness."

Subbuti replied, "But I haven't uttered a word about emptiness."

"True," the gods replied. "You have not spoken of emptiness, we have not heard of emptiness. This is true emptiness." And the showers of blossoms continued to fall.

If I had spoken of my emptiness or even been aware of it would it be emptiness?

Music needs the hollowness of the flute, letters, the blankness of the page, light, the void call a window, holiness, the absence of the self.

An old rabbi was lying ill in bed and his disciples were holding a whispered conversation at his bedside. They were extolling his unparalleled virtues.

"Not since the time of Solomon has there been one as wise as he," said one of them. "And his faith! It equals that of our father Abraham!" said another. "Surely his patience equals that of Job," said a third. 'Only in Moses can we find someone who conversed as intimately with God." said a fourth.

The rabbi seemed restless. When the disciples had gone his wife said to him, "Did you hear them sing your praises?"

"I did," said the rabbi.

"Then why are you so fretful?" said his wife.

"My modesty," complained the rabbi. "No one mentioned my modesty!"

He was indeed a saint who said.
"I am only four bare walls—with nothing inside."
No one could be fuller.

A ninety-two year old priest was venerated by everyone in town. When he appeared on the streets people would bow low, such was the man's reputation for holiness. He was also a member of the Rotary Club. Every time the Club met he would be there, always on time and always seated at his favourite spot in a corner of the room.

One day the priest disappeared. It was as if he vanished into thin air because, search as they might, the townsfolk could find no trace of him. The following month, however, when the Rotary Club met, there he was as usual, sitting in his corner.

"But, Father," everyone cried, "where have you been?" "In prison," said Father calmly. "In prison? for heaven's sake you couldn't hurt a fly! What happened?" "It's a long story," said the priest, "but, briefly, this is what happened: I bought myself a train ticket to the city and was waiting on the platform for the train to arrive when this stunningly beautiful girl appears on the arm of a policeman. She looks me over, turns to the cop and say, "He did it." And to tell you the truth I was so flattered, I pleaded guilty."

Four monks decided to go into silence for a month. They started out well enough but after the first day one monk said, "I wonder if I locked the door of my cell at the monastery before we set out."

Another monk said, "You fool! We decided to keep silence for a month and now you have gone and broken it!"

A third monk said, "What about you? You have broken it too!"

Said the fourth, "Thank God I'm the only one who hasn't spoken yet!"

THE SAINTS

A man walked into a doctor's office and said, "Doctor, I have this awful headache that never leaves me. Could you give me something for it?"

"I will," said the doctor, "But I want to check a few things out first. Tell me, do you drink a lot of liquor?"

"Liquor?" said the man indignantly, "I never touch the filthy stuff."

"How about smoking?"

"I think smoking is disgusting. I've never in my life touched tobacco."

"I'm a bit embarrassed to ask this, but... you know the way some men are.. do you do any running around at night?"

"Of course not. What do you take me for? I'm in bed every night by ten o'clock at the latest."

"Tell me," said the doctor, "this pain in the head you speak of, is it a sharp, shooting kind of pain?"

"Yes," said the man. "That's it—a sharp, shooting kind of pain."

"Simple, my dear fellow! Your trouble is you have your halo on too tight. All we need to do for you, is loosen it a bit."

The trouble with your ideals
is that, if you live up to all of them.
you become impossible to live with.

141

An influential British politician kept pestering Disraeli for a baronetcy. The Prime Minister could not see his way to obliging the man but he managed to refuse him without hurting his feelings. He said, 'I am sorry I cannot give you a baronetcy, but I can give you something better: you can tell your friends that I offered you the baronetcy and that you turned it down.

One day a bishop knelt before the altar and, in an outburst of religious fervour, began to beat his breast and exclaim, "I'm a sinner, have mercy on me! I'm a sinner, have mercy on me!"

The local priest, inspired by this example of humility, fell on his knees beside the bishop and began to beat his breast and say, "I'm a sinner, have mercy on me! I'm a sinner, have mercy on me!"

The sexton who happened to be in church at the time was so moved he could not restrain himself. He too fell on his knees, beat his breast, and cried out, "I'm a sinner, have mercy on me!"

Whereupon the bishop nudged the priest and, pointing towards the sexton, said with a smile, "Look who think he's a sinner!"

THE SAINTS

There was once an ascetic who lived a celibate life and made it his life's mission to fight against sex in himself and others.

In due course he died. And his disciple, who could not stand the shock, died a little after him. When the disciple reached the other world he couldn't believe what he saw: there was his beloved Master with the most extraordinarily beautiful woman seated on his lap!

He sense of shock faded when it occurred to him that his Master was being rewarded for his sexual abstinence on earth. He went up to him and said, "Beloved Master, now I know that God is just, for you are being rewarded in heaven for your austerities on earth."

The Master seemed annoyed. "Idiot!" he said, "this isn't heaven and I'm not being rewarded—She's being punished."

When the shoe fits the foot is forgotten;
When the belt fits the waist is forgotten;
When all things are in harmony the ego is forgotten.
Of what use, then, are your austerities?

The local priest was often seen talking to a comely woman of bad repute—and in public places too, to the great scandal of his congregation.

He was summoned by his bishop for a dressing down. When the bishop had done, the priest said, "Your Excellency, I have always held that it is better to talk to a pretty woman with one's thoughts set on God than to pray to God with one's thoughts fixed on a pretty woman."

When the monk goes to the tavern
the tavern becomes his cell.
When the drunk goes to a cell,
the cell becomes his tavern.

An earthquake hit the town and the Master was pleased to note how impressed his disciples were by his display of fearlessness.

When asked some days later what it meant to conquer fear, he reminded them of his own example. "Did you observe how, while everyone was running to and fro in panic, I sat still, calmly sipping water? Did any of you see my hand shake while I held the glass?"

"No," said a disciple. "But it wasn't water you were drinking, sir, but soya bean sauce."

* * *

Nisterus the Great, one of the holy Fathers of the Egyptian Desert, was one day walking in the desert with a large number of disciples who revered him as a man of God.

Suddenly a dragon appeared before them and they all ran away.

Many years later, as Nisterus lay dying, one of the disciples said to him, "Father, were you also frightened the day we saw the dragon?"

"No," said the dying man.

"Then why did you run away with the rest of us?"

"I thought it better to flee the dragon, so I would not have to flee from the spirit of vanity later.

When the Egyptian deserts were the abode of those holy men called the Fathers of the Desert a woman suffering from cancer of the breast went in search of one of them, a certain Abba Longinus, for the man had the reputation of a saint and a healer.

Now as the woman was walking along the sea, she came upon Longinus himself collecting firewood, and said, "Holy father, could you tell me where the servant of God Abba Longinus lives?"

Longinus said, "Why are you looking for that old fraud? Do not go to see him for he will only do you harm. What's your trouble?"

She told him what it was. He thereupon gave her his blessing and sent her on her way saying, "Go now, and God will surely make you whole again. Longinus would have been of no help to you at all."

So the woman went away, confident in the faith that she had been healed—which she was, before the month was over—and she died many years later quite unaware that it was Longinus who had healed her.

Once someone approached a disciple of the Muslim mystic Bahaudin Naqshband and said, "Tell me way your Master conceals his miracles. I have personally collected data that shows beyond any doubt that he has been present in more than one place at a time; that he healed people by the power of his prayers but tells them it was the work of nature; that he helped people in their troubles and then attributes it to their good luck. Why does he do this?"

"I know exactly what you are talking about," said the disciple, "for I have observed these things myself. And I think I can give you the answer to your question. First, the Master recoils from being the centre of attention. And secondly, he is convinced that once people develop an interest in the miraculous, they have no desire to learn anything of true spiritual value."

Laila and Rama were lovers, but too poor to get married as yet. They lived in different villages separated by a broad river that was infested with crocodiles.

One day Laila heard that her Rama was dangerously ill with no one to nurse him. She rushed to the river bank and pleaded with the boatman to take her across even though she did not have the money to pay him.

But the wicked boatman refused unless she agreed to sleep with him that night. The poor woman begged and pleaded but to no avail so, in sheer desperation, she consented to the boatman's terms.

When she finally got to Rama she found him near to death. But she stayed with him for a month and nursed him back to health. One day Rama asked how she had managed to cross the river. Being incapable of lying to her beloved, she told him the truth.

When Rama heard her tale he fell into a rage for he valued virtue more than life itself. He drove her out of the house and refused to look at her again.

THE SAINTS

Gessen was a Buddhist monk. He was also an exceptionally talented artist. Before he started work on any painting, however, he always demanded payment in advance. And his fees were exorbitant. So he came to be known as the Greedy Monk.

A geisha once sent for him to have a painting done. Gessen said, "How much will you pay me?" The girl happened to be entertaining a patron at that time. She said, "Any sum you ask for. But the painting must be done right now before me."

Gessen set to work at once and when the painting was completed he asked for the highest sum he had ever charged. As the geisha was giving him his money, she said to her patron, "This man is supposed to be a monk but all he thinks of is money. His talent is exceptional but he has a filthy, money-loving mind. How does one exhibit the canvas of a filthy-minded man like that? His work is good enough for my underclothing!"

With that she flung a petticoat at him and asked him to paint a picture on it. Gessen asked the usual question before he started the work: "How much will you give me?" "Oh, any sum you ask for," said the girl. Gessen named his price, painted the picture, shamelessly pocketed the money and walked away.

Many years later, quite by chance, someone found out why Gessen was so greedy for money. A devastating famine often struck his home province. The rich would do nothing to help the poor. So Gessen had secret barns built in the area and had them filled with grain for such emergencies.

No one knew where the grain came from or who the benefactor of the province was

Another reason why Gessen wanted money was the road leading to his village from the city many miles away. It was in such bad condition that ox-carts could not move on it; this caused much suffering to the aged and the infirm when they needed to get to the city. So Gessen had the road repaired.

The final reason was a meditation temple which Gessen's teacher had always desired to build but could not. Gessen built this temple as a token of gratitude to his revered teacher.

After the Greedy Monk had built the road, the temple and the barns, he threw away his paint and brushes, retired to the mountains to give himself to the contemplative life and never painted another canvas again.

A person's conduct generally shows
with the observer imagines it to show.

THE SAINTS

Two Irish navies were working on the road outside a house of prostitution.

Presently the local Protestant minister came along, pulled down his hat and walked into the building. Pat said to Mike, "Did you see that? What can you expect? He's a Protestant, isn't he?"

Soon after a rabbi arrived on the scene. He pulled his collar up and walked in too. Said Pat, "What a terrible example for a religious leader to give his people!"

Finally, who should pass by but a Catholic priest. He drew his cloak around his head and slipped into the building. Said Pat, "Now isn't it a terrible thing, Mike, to think that one of the girls must have taken ill?"

A man was fishing in the northern mountains. One day his guide took to telling him anecdotes about the bishop whose guide he had been the previous summer.

"Yes," the guide was saying, "he's a good man except for the language."

"Are you saying that the bishop swears?" asked the man.

"Oh, but of course, sir," said the guide. "Once he caught a fine salmon. Just as he was about the land it, the fish slipped off the hook, So I say to the bishop, "That's damned bad luck!" and the bishop, he looks me straight in the eye and he says, "Yes, it is indeed!' But that's the only time I heard the bishop use such language."

THE SAINTS

During the Meigi era two well-known teachers lived in Tokyo; as unlike each other as it was possible to be. One, Unsho, a Shingon teacher, was a man who meticulously observed every one of Buddha's precepts. He rose well before dawn, retired when the night was young, are nothing after the sun had passed its zenith and drank no intoxicating drinks. The other, Tanzan, was a philosophy professor at the Imperial Todai University. He observed no precepts for he ate when he felt like eating and slept even during the day time.

One day Unsho visited Tanzan and found him in his cups. This was quite scandalous since not even a drop is supposed to touch the tongue of a Buddhist.

"Hello, my friend," Tanzan exclaimed. "Will you come in and have a drink with me?"

Unsho was outraged. But he said in a controlled voice, "I never drink."

"One who does not drink is not human, surely," said Tanzan.

This time Unsho lost his temper. "Do you mean to say I am inhuman because I do not touch what the Buddha explicitly forbade? If I am not human, what am I?"

"A Buddha," said Tanzan happily.

Tanzan's manner of dying was as ordinary as was his manner of living. On the last day of his life he wrote sixty postcards, each of which read:

> I am departing from this world
> This is my last announcement.
> Tanzan. July 27, 1892.

He asked a friend to mail these cards for him, then quietly passed away.

The Sufi Junaid of Baghdad says, "The good-natured sensualist is better than the bad-tempered saint."

THE SAINTS

A family of five were enjoying their day at the beach. The children were bathing in the ocean and making castles in the sand when in the distance a little old lady appeared Her grey hair was blowing in the wind and her clothes were dirty and ragged. She was muttering something to herself as she picked up things from the beach and put them into a bag.

The parents called the children to their side and told them to stay away from the old lady. As she passed by, bending down every now and then to pick things up, she smiled at the family. But her greeting wasn't returned.

Many weeks later they learnt that the little old lady had made it her lifelong crusade to pick up bits of glass from the beach so children wouldn't cut their feet.

Wandering ascetics are common in India and a peasant mother had forbidden her son to have anything to do with them for, while some of them were reputed to be holy, others were known to be exploiters in disguise.

One day a mother looked out of her window and saw an ascetic surrounded by the village children. To her surprise, the man, quite unconscious of his dignity, was doing somersaults to entertain them. So impressed was she by the sight that she called out to her little boy and said, "Son, this one's a holy man. You may go out to him."

There was once a priest so holy that he never thought ill of anyone.

One day he sat down at a restaurant for a cup of coffee which was all he could take, it being a day of fast and abstinence, when, to his surprise, he saw a young member of his congregation devouring a massive steak at the next table.

"I trust I haven't shocked you, Father," said the young fellow with a smile.

"Ah! I take it that you forgot that today is a day of fast and abstinence," said the priest.

"No, no. I remembered it distinctly."

"Then you must be sick. The doctor has forbidden you to fast."

"Not at all. I'm in the pink of health."

At that, the priest raised his eyes to heaven and said, "What an example this younger generation is to us, Lord! Do you see how this young man here would rather admit his sins than tell a lie?"

Of the great Zen Master Rinzai it was said that each night the last thing he did before he went to bed was let out a great big belly laugh that resounded through the corridors and was heard in every building of the monastery grounds.

And the first thing he did when he woke at dawn was burst into peals of laughter so loud they woke up every monk no matter how deep his slumber.

His disciples asked him repeatedly to tell them why he laughed but he wouldn't. And when he died he carried the secret of his laughter with him to the grave.

The master was in an expansive mood so his disciples sought to learn from him the stages he had passed through in his quest for the divine.

"Good first led me by the hand," he said.' "into the Land of Action and there I dwelt for several years. Then He returned and led me to the Land of Sorrows: there I lived until my heart was purged of every inordinate attachment. That is when I found myself in the Land of Love whose burning flames consumed whatever was left in me of self. This brought me to the Land of Silence where the mysteries of life and death were bared before my wondering eyes."

"Was that the final stage of your quest?" they asked.

'No," The Master said, "One day God said, 'Today I shall take you to the innermost sanctuary of the Temple, to the heart of God himself.' And I was led to the Land of Laughter."

"Prisoner at the bar," said the Grand Inquisitor, "you are charged with encouraging people to break the laws, traditions and customs of our holy religion. How do you plead?"

"Guilty, your Honour."

"And with frequenting the company of heretics, prostitutes, public sinners, the extortionist tax-collectors, the colonial conquerors of our nation—in short, the excommunicated. How do you plead?"

"Guilty, your Honour."

"Finally, you are charged with revising, correcting, calling into question the sacred tenets of our faith. How do you plead?"

"Guilty, your Honour."

"What is your name, prisoner?"

"Jesus Christ, your Honour."

Some people are just as alarmed to see their religion practised as they are to hear it doubted.

THE SELF

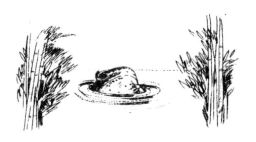

An elderly gentleman ran a curio and antique shop in a large city. A tourist once stepped in and got to talking with the old man about the many things that were stacked that shop.

Said the tourist, "What would you say is the strangest the most mysterious thing you have here?"

The old man surveyed the hundreds of curios, antiques, stuffed animals, shrunken heads, mounted fish and birds, archeological finds, deer heads... then turned to the tourist and said, "The strangest thing in this shop in unquestionably myself."

A teacher was giving a lecture on modern inventions.

"Can any of you mention something of importance that did not exist fifty years ago?" she asked.

One bright lad in the front row raised his hand eagerly and said, "Me!"

There is a revealing story of a monk living in the Egyptian desert who was so tormented by temptation that he could bear it no longer. So he decided to abandon his cell and go somewhere else.

As he was putting on his sandals to carry out his resolve he saw another monk not far from where he stood who was also putting his sandals on.

"Who are you?" he asked the stranger.

"I am your self," was the reply. "If it is on my account that you are leaving this place, I would have you know that no matter where you go I shall go with you."

Said a despairing client to the psychiatrist, "No matter where I go I have to take myself along—and that spoils everything."

Both what you run away from—and what you yearn for—is within you.

A seeker, in search of a Master who would lead him to the path of holiness, came to an ashram presided over by a guru who, in addition to having a great reputation for holiness, was also a fraud. But the seeker did not know this.

"Before I accept you as my disciple," said the guru, "I must test your obedience. There is a river flowing by the ashram that is infested with crocodiles. I want you to wade across the river."

So great was the faith of the young disciple that he did just that: he walked across the river crying, "All praise to the power of my guru!" To the guru's astonishment the man walked to the other bank and back unharmed.

This convinced the guru that he was more of a saint than he himself had imagined, so he decided to give all his disciples a demonstration of his power and thereby enhance his reputation for holiness. He stepped into the river crying, "All praise to me! All praise to me!" The crocodiles promptly seized him and devoured him.

The devil, transformed into an angel of light, appeared to one of the holy Fathers of the Desert and said, "I am the Angel Gabriel and I have been sent to thee by the Almighty."

The monk replied, "Think again. You must have been sent to someone else. I have done nothing to deserve the visit of an angel."

With that the devil vanished and never again dared come anywhere near the monk.

A tourist in Japan discovered, when he visited the golf links, that most of the good caddies were women.

One day he arrived late at the course and had to take a young lad of ten as caddie. He was a tiny fellow, knew next to nothing about the course or the game and he spoke only three words of English.

Thanks to those three words, however, the tourist made him his caddie for the rest of his stay. After each host, regardless of the result, the little fellow would stamp his foot and shout with feeling, "Damned good shot!"

A woman was deeply hurt by the behaviour of her fifteen year old son. Each time they went out together he would walk on ahead of her. Was he ashamed of her? One day she asked him.

"Oh, Mom, no," was his embarrassed reply. "It's just that you look so young that I'm worried my friends will suspect I have a new girl friend."

Her hurt vanished as if by magic.

An elderly man stood at the door with a piece of cake in his hand. "My wife is eighty-six today," he said, "and she wants you to have a piece of her birthday cake." The cake was received gratefully, particularly because the man had walked nearly half a mile to deliver it.

An hour later he was back. "Is anything the matter?" he was asked.

"Well," he replied sheepishly, "Agatha sent me back to say she's only eighty-five."

A rooster was scratching around in the stall of a large farm horse.

When the horse began to get restless and started moving around, the rooster looked up at him and said, "We'd, both of us, better be careful, brother, or we are likely to step on each other's toes."

Guess what the ant said to the elephant when Noah was lining up all the animals to get them into the ark.

He said, "Stop pushing!"

A flea decided to move with his family into the ear of an elephant. So he shouted, "Mr. Elephant, sir, my family and I plan to move into your ear. I think it only fair to give you a week to think the matter over and let me know if you have any objection."

The elephant, who was not even aware of the existence of the flea went his placid way so, after conscientiously waiting for a week, the flea assumed the elephant's consent and moved in.

A month later Mrs. Flea decided that the elephant's ear was not a healthy place to live in and urged her husband to move out at least a month so as not to hurt the elephant's feelings.

Finally, he put it as tactfully as he could: "Mr. Elephant, sir, we plan to move to other quarters. This has nothing at all to do with you, of course, because your ear is spacious and warm. It is just that my wife would rather live next door to her friends at the buffalo's foot. It you have any objection to our moving, do let me know in the course of the next week."

The elephant said nothing, so the flea changed residence with a clear conscience.

The universe is not aware of your existence! Relax!

The choir was going through its final rehearsal in the midst of pandemonium because the stage crew was busy putting the finishing touches to the stage.

When one young fellow began hammering away so loudly that the din became intolerable, the conductor stopped the singing and looked at him pleadingly.

"Go right ahead with the singing, conductor," the merry worker said. "They're not disturbing me."

A woman stepped out of her shower stark naked and was about to reach for her towel when she saw, to her horror, that there was a man on a scaffolding washing her window and eyeing her appreciatively.

So shocked was she by the unexpected apparition that she stood transfixed to the ground, gaping at the man.

"What's the matter, lady?" the fellow asked cheerfully "Have you never seen a window cleaner before?"

There was once a scientist who discovered the art of reproducing himself so perfectly that it was impossible to tell the reproduction from the original. One day he learnt that the Angel of Death was searching for him so he produced a dozen copies of himself. The Angel was at a loss to know which of the thirteen specimens before him was the scientist, so he left them all alone and returned to heaven.

But not for long, for, being an expert in human nature, the angel came up with a clever device. He said, "Sir, you must be a genius to have succeeded in making such perfect reproductions of yourself. However, I have discovered a flaw in your work, just one tiny little flaw."

The scientist immediately jumped out and shouted, "Impossible. Where is the flaw?"

"Right here," said the angel, as he picked up the scientist from among the reproductions and carried him off.

There was an old Arab Judge who was known for his sagacity. One day a shopkeeper came to him to complain that goods from his shop were being stolen but he was unable to catch the thief.

The judge commanded the door of the shop to be taken off its hinges, carried to the market-place and given fifty lashes because it had failed to do its duty of keeping the thief out of the store.

A large crowd collected to see this strange sentence being carried out. When the lashes had been administered, the judge stooped and asked the door who the thief was. Then he applied his ear to the door, the better to hear what it had to say.

When he stood up he announced, "The door declares that the burglaries have been committed by a man who has a cobweb on the top of his turban." Instantly the hand of the one man in the crowd went up to his turban. His house was searched and the stolen goods recovered.

All it takes
is a word of flattery
or criticism
to uncover the ego.

An old woman died and was taken to the Judgement Seat by the angels. While examining her records however, the judge could not find a single act of charity performed by her except for a carrot she had once given to a starving beggar.

Such, however, is the power of a single deed of love that it was decreed that she be taken up to heaven on the strength of that carrot. The carrot was brought to court and given to her. The moment she caught hold of it, it began to rise as if pulled by some invisible string lifting her up towards the sky.

A beggar appeared. He clutched on to the hem of her garment and was lifted along wit her; a third person caught hold of the beggar's foot and was lifted too. Soon there was a long line of persons being lifted up to heaven by that carrot. And, strange as it may seem, the woman did not feel the weight of all those people who held on to her; in fact, since she was looking heavenward, she did not see them.

Higher and higher they rose until they were almost near the heavenly gates. That is when the woman looked back to catch a last glimpse of the earth and saw this whole rain of people behind her.

She was indignant! She gave an imperious wave of her hand and shouted, "Off! Off, all of you! This carrot is mine.

In making her imperious gesture she let go of the carrot for a moment – and down she fell with the entire train.

There is only one cause for every evil on earth
"This belongs to me!"

A wood-carver called Ching had just finished work on a bell-frame. Everyone who saw it marvelled for it seemed to be the work of spirits. When the Duke of Lu saw it, he asked, "What sort of genius is yours that you could make such a thing?"

The wood-carver replied, "Sire, I am only a simple workman. I am no genius. But there is one thing. When I am going to make a bell-frame I meditate for three days to calm my mind. When I have meditated for three days I think no more about rewards or emoluments. When I have meditated for five days I no longer think of praise or blame, skillfulness or awkwardness. When I have meditated for seven days I suddenly forget my limbs, my body!; no, I forget my very self. I lose consciousness of the court and my walk roundings. Only my skill remains. In that state I walk into the forest and examine each tree until I find one in which I see the bell-frame in all its perfection. Then my hands go to the task. Having set my self aside, nature meets nature in the work that is performed through me. This no doubt is the reason why everyone says that the finished product is the work of spirits."

Said a world famous violinist about his success in playing Beethoven's Violin concerto: "I have splendid music, a splendid violin and a splendid bow. All I need to do is bring them together and get out of the way."

A disciple came to Maruf Karkhi, the Muslim Master, and said, "I have been talking to people about you. The Jews say you are one of their own. The Christians consider you to be one of their saints. And the Muslims look upon you as a glory to Islam."

Maruf replied, "That's what they say here in Baghdad. When I lived in Jerusalem the Jews dubbed me a Christian: the Christians, a Muslim: and the Muslims, a Jew."

"Then what are we to think of you?"

"Think of me as a man who said this about himself: Those who do not understand me revere me. Those who revile me do not understand me either."

If you think you are what your friends and enemies say you are, you obviously do not know yourself.

A woman in a coma was dying. She suddenly had a feeling that she was taken up to heaven and stood before the Judgement Seat.

"Who are you?" a Voice said to her.
"I'm the wife of the mayor," she replied.
"I did not ask you whose wife you are but who you are."
"I'm the mother of four children."
"I did not ask whose mother you are, but who you are."
"I'm a schoolteacher."
"I did not ask you what your profession is but who you are."

And so it went. No matter what she replied, she did not seem to give a satisfactory answer to do question. "Who are you?"

"I'm a Christian."
"I did not ask what your religion is but who are you."
"I'm the one who went to church every day and always helped the poor and needy."
"I did not ask you what you did not but who you are."

She evidently failed the examination for she was sent back to earth. When she recovered from her illness she determined to find out who she was. And that made all the difference.

Your duty is to be. Not to be somebody, not to be nobody—for therein lies greed and ambition—not to be this or that—and thus become conditioned—but just to be.

THE SELF

A worried looking fellow walks into the psychiatrist's office smoking pot and wearing love-beads, bell-bottom trousers frayed at the ends and shoulder-length hair.

The psychiatrist says, "You claim you are not a hippie. Then how do you explain the clothes, the hair, the pot?"

"That's what I'm here to find out, doctor."

To know things is to be learned.
To know others is to be wise.
To know the self is to be enlightened.

A student walked up to the clerk at the language laboratory and said "May I have a blank tape, please?"

"What language are you studying?" asked the clerk.

"French," aid the student.

"Sorry, we don't have any blank tapes in French."

"Well, do you have any blank tapes in English?"

"Yes, we do."

"Good. I'll take one of those."

It makes as much sense to speak of a blank tape as being French or English as it does to speak of a person as being French or English. French or English is your conditioning, not you.

A baby born of American parents and adopted by Russian parents: has no notion he has been adopted and grows up to be a great patriot and poet who gives expression to the collective unconscious of the Russian soul and the aspirations of Mother Russia: is he Russian? American? Neither.

Find out who/what you are.

THE SELF

"What is that door doing under your arm?"
"It's the front door of my house. I lost the key, and am taking it to have a fresh key made."
"Make sure you don't lose the door now, or you won't be able to enter your house."
"Well, I left a window open just to be on the safe side."

The Zen Master, Bankei, is said to have founded no school. He left no works and no disciples. He was like a bird that leaves no trace of its flight across the sky.

Of him it was said, "When he entered the forest not a blade of grass stirred; when he entered the water not a ripple was made."

He did not encumber the earth. No feat of daring, no conquest or accomplishment or spirituality is to be compared with this: not to encumber the earth.

A man came to Buddha with an offering of flowers in his hands. Buddha looked up at him and said, "Drop it!"

He couldn't believe he was being asked to drop the flowers. But then it occurred to him that he was probably being invited to drop the flowers he had in his left hand, since to offer something with one's left hand was considered inauspicious and impolite. So he dropped the flowers that his left hand held.

Still Buddha said, "Drop it!"

This time he dropped all the flowers and stood empty-handed before Buddha who once again said, with a smile, "Drop it!"

Perplexed, the man asked, "What is it I am supposed to drop?"

"Not the flowers, son, but the one who brought them," was Buddha's reply.

There was a Guru who was looked upon by all as Wisdom Incarnate. Each day he would discourse on various aspects of the spiritual life and it was obvious to all that never had anyone surpassed this man for the variety, the depth and the enticing quality of his teaching.

Again and again his disciples would ask him about the source from which he drew this inexhaustible store of wisdom. He told them it was all written down in a book that they would inherit after he was dead.

The day after his death, the disciples found the book exactly where he told them it would be. There was only one page in that book and only one sentence on that page. It read: "Understand the difference between the container and the content and the fount of Wisdom shall be open to you."

A tale from the Upanishads:

The sage Uddalaka taught his son Svetaketu to see the One behind the appearance of the many. He did this by means of several parables like the one that follows:

One day he said to his son, "Put this salt in water and come back to me in the morning."

The boy did as the was told and the next day his father said, "Please bring me the salt you put in the water yesterday."

"I cannot find it," said the boy. "It has dissolved."

"Taste the water from this side of the dish," said Uddalaka. "What taste does it have?"

"Salt."

"Sip it in the middle. What is it like?"

"Salt."

"Sip it from the other side of the dish. What is it like?" Salt

"Throw it away," said the father.

The boy did so and observed that after the water had evaporated the salt reappeared. Then Uddalaka said, "You cannot perceive God here, my son, but in fact he is here."

Those who seek for enlightenment fail to find it for they fail to understand that the object of the search is the seeker. God, like beauty, is in the I of the beholder.

LOVE

"My friend isn't back from the battlefield, sir. Request permission to go out and get him."

"Permission refused," said the officer. "I don't want you to risk your life for a man who is probably dead."

The soldier went, all the same, and, an hour later, came back mortally wounded, carrying the corpse of his friend.

The officer was furious. "I told you he was dead. Now I've lost both of you. Tell me, was it worth going out there to bring in a corpse?"

The dying man replied, "Oh, it was, sir. When I got to him he was still alive. And he said to me, 'Jack, I was sure you'd come."

A little girl was dying of a disease from which her eight-year-old brother had recovered some time before.

The doctor said to the boy, "Only a transfusion of your blood will save the life of your sister. Are you ready to give her your blood?"

The eyes of the boy widened in fear. He hesitated for a while, then finally said, "OK, doctor. I'll do it."

An hour after the transfusion was completed the boy asked hesitantly, "Say, doctor, when do I die?" It was only then that the doctor understood the momentary fear that had seized the child: he thought that in giving his blood he was giving his life for his sister.

A disciple very much wanted to renounce the world but he claimed that his family loved him too much to let him go.

"Love?" said his guru. "That isn't love at all. Listen..." And he revealed a yogic secret to the disciple whereby he could simulate the state of death. The next day the man was dead to all outward appearances and the house rang with the cries and wailing of his family.

The guru then showed up and told the weeping family that he had the power to bring the man back of life it someone could be found to die in his place. Any volunteers?

To the "corpse's" astonishment every member of the family began to bring forth reasons why it was necessary to keep their own lives. His wife summed up the sentiments of all with the words. "There's really no need for anyone to take his place. We'll manage without him.

Three grown-ups were having morning coffee in the kitchen while the children played on the floor. The conversation turned on what they would do it danger threatened and each of the grown-ups said that the first thing they would do was to save the children.

Suddenly the safety valve of the pressure cooker burst, creating an explosion of steam in the room. Within seconds everyone was out of the kitchen—except for the kids playing on the floor.

At the funeral of a very wealthy man a stranger was seen mourning and weeping as loudly as the others.

The officiating priest walked up to him and asked, "Are you, perhaps, a relative of the deceased?"

"No."

"Then why are you crying?"

"That's why."

All grief—no matter what the occasion—is for the self.

* * *

When a factory was burning down, the aged owner of the building was there weeping aloud at his loss.

"Dad, what are you weeping for?" said his son, "Have you forgotten that we sold the factory four days ago?"

That instantly stopped the old man's tears.

A saleswoman sold a brightly coloured pair of trousers to a lad who seemed delighted with his purchase.

The next day he was back to say he wanted to return the trousers. His reason, "My girlfriend does not like them."

A week later he was back again, all smiles, and wanting to buy the trousers. "Has your girl changed her mind?" asked the saleswoman.

"Nope," said the young fellow. "I've changed the girl."

Mother: "What does your girlfriend like in you."

"She thinks I'm handsome, talented, clever and a good dancer."

"And what do you like about her?"

"She thinks I'm handsome, talented, clever and a good dancer."

𝕿wo women friends met after many years.

"Tell me," said one, "What happened to your son?"

"My son? The poor, poor lad!" sighed the other: What an unfortunate marriage he made—to a girl who won't do a stitch of work in the house. She won't cook, she won't sew, she won't wash or clean. All she does is sleep and loaf and read in bed. The poor boy even has to bring her breakfast in bed, would you believe it?"

"That's awful! And what about your daughter?"

"Ah—now she's the lucky one! She married an angel. He won't let her do a thing in the house. He has servants to do the cooking and sewing and washing and cleaning. And each morning he brings her breakfast in bed, would you believe it? All she does is sleep for as long as she wishes and spends the rest of the day relaxing and reading in bed."

"Do you think you will be able to give my daughter what she wants?" a man asked a suitor.

"I certainly do, sir. She says that all she wants is me."

No one would call it love if what she wanted was money. Why is it love if what she wants is you?

When Robert, a fourteen-year-old lad fell in love with his fourteen-year-old neighbour, he sold off everything he had and even took on odd jobs to earn enough money to buy his sweetheart the expensive watch she wanted. His parents were dismayed but decided it was best to say nothing.

The day for the purchase arrived and Robert returned from his shopping expedition without spending his money. This is the explanation he gave: "I took her to the jeweller's and she said she didn't want the watch after all. She fancied other things more, like a bracelet, a necklace, a gold ring.

"While she was moving around the shop making up her mind I remembered what our teacher once told us, that before getting something we must ask ourselves what we wanted it for. That's when I realized that I did not really want her after all, so I walked out of the shop and came away."

A little boy was heartbroken to find his pet turtle lying on its back, lifeless and still, beside the pond.

His father did his best to console him: "Don't cry, son, We'll arrange a lovely funeral for Mr. Turtle. We'll make him a little coffin all lined in silk and get the undertaker to make a headstone for his grave, with Mr. Turtle's name carved on it. Then we'll have fresh flowers placed on the grave each day and make a little picket fence to go all around it."

The little boy dried his eyes and became enthusiastic about the project. When all was ready the cortege was formed— father, mother, maid and child chief mourner—and began to move solemnly towards the pond to bring in the body. But the body had vanished.

Suddenly they spied Mr. Turtle emerging from the depths of the pond and swimming around merrily. The little boy stared at his friend in bitter disappointment, then said, "Let's kill him."

It isn't really you I care about
but the thrill I get from loving you.

LOVE

A nun in search of enlightenment made a wooden statue of Buddha and covered it with a fine gold leaf. It was very pretty and everywhere she went she carried it with her.

Years passed and, still carrying her statue, the nun settled down in a small temple where there were many statues of Buddha, each with its own altar.

She began to burn incense before her golden Buddha each day but discovered, to her dismay, that some of the smoke wandered off to the neighbouring altars.'

So she made a paper funnel through which the smoke would ascend to her Buddha. This blackened the nose of the golden status and made it very ugly.

Fredrich Wilhelm who ruled Prussia in the early eighteenth century was known to be a short-tempered man. He also detested ceremony. He would walk the streets of Berlin unaccompanied and if anyone happened to displease him—a not infrequent occurrence—he would not hesitate to use his waling stick on the hapless victim.

Not surprisingly when people saw him at a distance they would quietly leave the vicinity. Once Fredrich came pounding down a street when a Berliner caught sigh of him—but too late, so his attempt to withdraw into a doorway was foiled.

"You there!" said Fredrich. "Where are you going?"

The man began to shake. "Into this house, your Majesty."

"Is it your house?"

"No, your Majesty."

"A friend's house?"

"No, your Majesty."

"Then why are you entering it?"

The man now began to fear that he would be taken for a burglar. So he blurted out the truth. "To avoid your Majesty."

"Why would you wish to avoid me?"

"Because I am afraid of your Majesty."

At this Fredrich Wilhelm became lived with rage. Siezing the poor man by the shoulders he shook him violently crying, "How dare you fear me! I am your ruler. You are supposed to love me! Love me, wretch! Love me!"

A massively built woman strode into the registrar's office, slamming the door shut behind her.

"Did you or did you not issue this licence for me to marry Jacob Jacobson?" she said, slamming the document on the table.

The registrar inspected the document closely through his thick glasses. "Yes, ma'am, I believe I did. Why?"

"Because," said the woman, "he's escaped. What are you going to do about it?"

After a heated argument with his wife a man said, "Why can't we live peacefully like our two dogs who never fight?"

"No, they don't," his wife agreed. "But tie them together and see what happens!"

An Arabian princess had set her heart on marrying one of her slaves. Nothing the king said or did succeeded in moving the girl from her resolve. And none of the king's advisers could tell him what to do.

Finally a wise old hakim appeared at court and, on hearing of the king's predicament, said, "Your Majesty is ill advised for if you forbid the girl to marry she will only resent you and be more attracted to the salve."

"Then tell me what to do ," cried the king.

The hakim suggested a plan of action.

The king was sceptical but decided to give it a try. He sent for the young woman and said, "I am going to put your love for this man to the test: you will be locked up in a tiny cell with your lover for thirty days and nights. If at the end of that period you still wish to marry him, you shall have my consent."

The princess, beside herself with joy, hugged her father and delightedly agreed to the test. All went well for a couple of days but boredom soon set in. Within a week she was pining for other company and exasperated at her lover's every word and action. After two weeks she was so sick of the man, she took to screaming and pounding on the door of the cell. When she was finally let out she flung her arms around her father in gratitude for having saved her from the man she had now come to abhor.

Living apart makes living together easier.
Without distance one cannot relate.

A teacher observed that one of the little boys in her class was pensive and withdrawn.

"What are you worried about?" she asked.

"My parents," he replied. "Dad works all day to keep me clothed and fed sent to the best school in town. And he's working overtime to be able to send me to college. Mom spends all day cooking and cleaning and ironing and shopping so I have nothing to worry about."

"Why, then, are you worried?"

"I'm afraid they might try to escape."

A Sunday school teacher told her children she was going to write their names on the blackboard. After each name she would write the one thing that particular child was the most grateful for.

One little boy was thinking hard when his name went on the board. When he was asked what should go after his name, he finally said, "Mother."

So that's what the teacher wrote. She was starting to write the next name when the boy began to wave his hand frantically.

"Yes?" said the teacher.

"Please cancel MOTHER," said the little boy, "and write DOG."

Why not?

LOVE

A man offered to pay a sum of money to his twelve-year-old daughter if she mowed the lawn. The girl went at the task with great zest and by evening the whole lawn had been beautifully mowed—well, everything except a large uncut patch of grass in one corner.

When the man said he couldn't pay the sum agreed upon because the whole lawn hadn't been mowed, the girl said she was ready to forego the money, but would not cut the grass in the patch.

Curious to find out why, he checked the uncut patch. There, right in the centre of the patch, sat a large toad. The girl had been too tender-hearted to run over it with the lawn-mower.

Where there is love, there is disorder.
Perfect order would make the world a graveyard.

A small crowd collected around the speaker at a street corner. "Come the revolution," he was saying, "everyone will drive around in big black limousines. Come the revolution, everyone will have a telephone in the kitchen. Come the revolution everyone will possess a plot of land they can call their own."

A voice from the crowd protested, "I don't want to own a big black limousine or a plot of land or a phone in the kitchen."

"Come the revolution," said the speaker, "You'll do as you're damned well told."

If you want a perfect world, get rid of the people.

One day Abraham invited a beggar to his tent for a meal. When grace was being said the man began to curse God, declaring he could not bear to hear His Name.

Seized with indignation, Abraham drove the blasphemer away.

When he was at his prayers that night, God said to him, "This man has cursed and reviled me for fifty years and yet I have given him food to eat every day. Could you not put up with him for a single meal?"

200

An old woman in the village was said to be receiving divine apparitions. The local priest demanded proof of their authenticity. "When God next appears to you," he said, "ask Him to tell you my sins which are known to Him alone. That should be evidence enough."

The woman returned a month later and the priest asked if God had appeared to her again. She said He had. "Did you put the question to him?"

"I did."

"And what did He say?"

"He said, "Tell your priest I have forgotten his sins."

Is it possible
that all of the horrible things you have done
have been forgotten by everyone
—except yourself?

201

Once some of the elders were in Scete and Abbot John the Dwarf was with them.

While they were dining, a priest, a very old man, got up and attempted to serve them. But no one would take so much as a cup of water from him except John the Dwarf.

The others were somewhat shocked about this and later said to him, "How is it that you considered yourself worthy to accept the service of that holy man?"

He replied, "Well, when I offer people a drink of water I'm happy if they take it. Did you expect me to sadden the old man by depriving him of the joy of giving me something?"

LOVE

When an eight-year-old girl spent her pocket money to buy her mother a gift, her mother was grateful and happy for a mother and housewife generally gets much work and little appreciation.

The girl seemed to have understood this for she said, "It's because you work so hard, mother, and no one appreciates it."

The woman said, "Your father works hard too."

Said the girl, "Yes, but he doesn't make a fuss about it."

An old pilgrim was making his way to the Himalayan mountains in the bitter cold of winter when it began to rain.

An innkeeper said to him, "How will you ever get there in this kind of weather, my good man?"

The old man answered cheerfully, "My heart got there first, so it's easy for the rest of me to follow."

Jeremiah was in love with a very tall woman. Each night he would walk her home from work and each night he longed to kiss her but was too shy to ask.

One night he summoned up the courage. "Will you let me kiss you?" She was agreeable. But Jeremiah was exceptionally small in stature, so they looked around for something he could stand on. They found an abandoned smithy with an anvil in it that gave Jeremiah just the height he needed.

After they had walked on for half a mile or so, Jeremiah said, "Could I have just one more kiss, darling?"

"No," said the woman. "I've given you one. That's enough for tonight."

Jeremiah said, "Then why didn't you stop me from carrying this damned anvil?"

Love bears a burden and feels no burden!

LOVE

A Caliph of Baghdad named Al-Mamun owned a beautiful Arabian horse. A tribesman called Omah was eager to buy the horse so he offered many camels in exchange for it, but Al-Mamun would not part with the animal. This so angered Omah that he decided to get the horse by trickery.

Knowing that Al-Mamun would ride his horse along a certain road, he lay down beside the road disguised as a beggar who was very ill. Now Al-Mamun was a kindhearted man so when he saw the beggar he felt sorry for him, dismounted and offered to carry him to a sarai.

"Alas!" cried the beggar, "I have been without food for days and do not have the energy to rise." So Al-Mamun tenderly lifted the man on to his horse meaning to mount after him. No sooner was the disguised beggar in the saddle than he galloped away with Al-Mamun giving chase on foot, shouting to him to stop. After Omah had put a safe distance between his pursuer and himself he stopped and turned around.

"You have stolen my horse," shouted Al-Mamun. "I have one request to make of you."

"What is it?" Omah shouted back.

"That you tell no one how you came into possession of the horse."

"Why not?"

"Because some day a man who is really ill may be lying by the roadside and, if your trick is known, people will pass him by and fail to help him."

205

It was time for the monsoon rains to begin and a very old man was digging holes in his garden.

"What are you doing?" his neighbour asked.

"Planting mango trees." was the reply.

"Do you expect to eat mangoes from those trees?"

"No, I won't live long enough for that. But others will. It occurred to me the other day that all my life I have enjoyed mangoes planted by other people. This is my way of showing them my gratitude."

✳ ✳ ✳

Diogenes was standing at a street corner one day laughing like a man out of his mind.

"What are you laughing about?" a passerby asked.

"Do you see that stone in the middle of the street? Since I got here this morning ten people have stumbled on it and cursed it. But not one of them took the trouble to remove it so others wouldn't stumble."

LOVE

A guru asked his disciples how they could tell when the night had ended and the day begun.

One said, "When you see an animal in the distance and can tell whether it is a cow or a horse."

"No," said the guru.

"When you look at a tree in the distance and can tell if it is a neem three or a mango tree."

"Wrong again," said the guru.

"Well, then, what is it?" asked the disciples.

"When you look into the face of any man and recognize your brother in him: when you look into the face of any woman and recognize in her your sister. If you cannot do this, no matter what time it is by the sun it is still night."

A friend came to the famous essayist Charles Lamb and said, "I want to introduce you to Mr. So-and-so."

"No, thank you," said Lamb. "I don't like the man."

"But you don't even know him!"

"I know. That is why I don't like him," said Lamb.

"When it comes to people, I know what I like."
"You mean you like what you know!"

It intrigued the congregation to see their rabbi disappear each week on the eve of the sabbath. They suspected he was secretly meeting the Almighty, so they deputed one of their number to follow him.

This is what the man saw: the rabbi disguised himself in peasant clothes and served a paralysed Gentile woman in her cottage, cleaning out the room and preparing a sabbath meal for her.

When the spy got back the congregation asked, "Where did the rabbi go? Did he ascend to heaven?"

"No," the man replied, "he went even higher."

LOVE

When Earl Mountbatten, the last Viceroy of India announced that his nephew, Prince Philip, was engaged to Princess Elizabeth, Mahatma Gandhi said to him, "I am delighted that your nephew is going to marry the future queen. I should like to give them a wedding present, but what can I give them? I have nothing."

"You have your spinning wheel," said the Viceroy. " "Get to work and spin them something."

Gandhi made them a tablecloth which Mountbatten sent to Princess Elizabeth with this note: "This you lock up with the crown jewels."

...for it was spun by a man who said: "The British must depart as friends."

There was an old Sufi who earned his living by selling all sorts of odds and ends. It seemed as if the man had no judgement because people would frequently pay him in bad coins and he would accept them without a word of protest, or people would claim they had paid him when they hadn't and he accepted their word for it.

When it was time for him to die, he raised his eyes to heaven and said, "Oh, Allah! I have accepted many bad coins from people, but never once did I judge them in my heart. I just assumed that they were not aware of what they did I am a bad coin too. Please do not judge me."

And a Voice was heard that said, "How is it possible to judge someone who has not judged others?"

Marry can do loving deeds
Rare is the person who can think loving thoughts.

LOVE

The family was gathered at dinner. The oldest boy announced he was going to marry the girl across the street.

"But her family didn't leave her a penny," objected his father.

"And she hasn't' saved a cent," added mother.

"She doesn't know a thing about football," said junior.

"I've never seen a girl with such funny hair," said sister.

"All she does is read novels," said uncle.

"And she does is read novels," said uncle.

"And such poor taste in she choice of her clothes," said aunt.

"But she isn't sparing of the powder and the paint," said grandma.

"True," said the boy. "But she has one supreme advantage over all of us."

"What's that?" everyone wanted to know.

"She has no family!"

Abbot Anastasius had a book of very fine parchment which was worth twenty pence. It contained both the Old and New Testaments in full. Once a certain monk came to visit him and, seeing the book, made off with it. So that day when Anastasius went to his scripture reading he found that it had gone and knew at once that the monk had taken it. But he did not send after him for fear that he might add the sin of perjury to that of theft

Now the monk went into the city to sell the book. He wanted eighteen pence for it. The buyer said, "Give me the book so that I may find out if it is worth much money." With that, he took the book to the holy Anastasius and said, "Father, take a look at this and tell me if you think it is worth as much as eighteen pence." Anastasius said, "Yes, it is a fine book. And at eighteen pence it is a bargain."

So the buyer went back to the monk sand said, "Here is your money. I showed the book to Father Anastasius and he said it was worth eighteen pence."

The monk was stunned. "Was that all he said? Did he say nothing else?"

"No, he did not say a word more than that."

"Well, I have changed my mind and don't want to sell the book after all."

Then he went back to Anastasius and begged him with many tears to take the book back but Anastasius said gently, "No, brother, keep it. It is my present to you." But the monk said, "If you do not take it back I shall have no peace."

After that the monk dwelt with Anastasius for the rest of his life.

Jitoku was a fine poet and he had made up his mind
to study Zen. So he got himself an appointment with
the Master Ekkei in Kyoto. He went to the Master full of
expectations but as soon as he entered he received a
whack. He was shocked and humiliated. Never before
had anyone dared to strike him. But since it was the strict
Zen rule never to say or do anything unless invited by
the Master, he silently walked out. He went over to where
Dokuon, the chief disciple, lived, told him the whole story
and also his intention to challenge the Master to a duel.

"But the Master was being kind to you," said Dokuon.
"Throw yourself into the practice of zazen and you will se
that for yourself."

That is exactly what Jitoku did. For three days and nights,
such was the intensity of his efforts that he achieved an
ecstatic enlightenment quite beyond anything he could
have imagined. This satori of his was approved by Ekkei.

Once again Jitoku called on Dokuon, thanked him for his
advice and said, "If it hadn't been for your good sense I
would never have had this transforming experience. And
as for the Master, I see now that his blow wasn't hard
enough!"

Muso, one of the most illustrious Masters of his day, was travelling in the company of a disciple. They came to a river and boarded a ferry. Just as it was about to leave the shore a drunken samurai ran up and jumped into the overloaded boat, nearly sinking it. Then he staggered around wildly, endangering the safety of the frail vessel, so the boatman begged him to stay quiet.

"We're stuffed in here like gooseberries in a bottle." said the samurai raucously. Suddenly he saw Muso and shouted, "Here! Let's throw the holy man over board!"

"Please be patient," said Muso. "We'll soon be across."

"What? Me be patient?" he shouted wildly. "Look! if you don't jump off, I'll throw you overboard this minute."

The Master's calm demeanour in the face of these threats so enraged the samurai that he walked up to Muso and struck him across the face, drawing blood. The disciple had had enough. He was a powerful man and he said. "After what he had done, he shall not live."

"Why get so upset about a trifle?" said Muso with a smile. "It is on occasions like this that our training is put to the test. You must remember that patience is more than just a word." Then he composed a little poem that ran:

"The beater and the beaten:
mere actors in a play
that is as short-lived as a dream."

214

Seven crazy men were invited to festivities in a neighbouring village. More than mildly intoxicated, they were staggering home towards their own village at night when it began to rain.

So they settled down for the night under a large banyan tree.

When they woke up the following morning they rent the air with mourning and wailing. "What's the matter?" asked a passerby.

""Last night, we huddled together under this tree and fell asleep, sir," said one of the crazy men. "On walking up this morning we find our limbs all intertwined and we cannot distinguish the owners."

"Easily solved," said the traveller. "Give me a pin." He jabbed the pin sharply into the first leg he saw. "Ouch!" said one of the men. "There," said the traveller to the man, "that leg is yours." Then he pricked an arm. "Ouch!" said another, identifying himself as the owner of the arm. And so on, till the limbs were all disentangled and the crazy men went merrily back to their village none the worse for their experience.

When your heart responds instinctively to other people's joys and sorrows you will know you have lost your self and attained the experience of your "one-body-ness" with the human race— and love has finally arrived.

TRUTH

Truth is not found in formulas...

A man was drinking tea with a friend in a restaurant. He looked long and hard at his cup, then said with a resigned sigh, "Ah, my friend, life is like a cup of tea."

The other pondered this for a while, looked long and hard at his own cup, then asked, "Why? Why is life like a cup of tea?"

The man said, "How should I know? Am I an intellectual?"

or in figures...

"Prisoner at the bar," said the judge, "I find you guilty on twenty-three counts. I therefore sentence you to a total of one hundred and seventy-five years."

The prisoner was an old man. He burst into tears. The judge's facial expression softened. "I did not mean to be harsh," he said. "I know the sentence I have imposed is a very severe one. You don't really have to serve the whole of it."

The prisoner's eyes brightened with hope.

"That's right," said the judge. "Just do as much as you can!"

A bishop had decreed that woman housekeepers for priests should be at least fifty years of age. He was startled, in the visitation of his diocese, to discover a priest who thought he was observing the law by keeping two housekeepers, each of whom was twenty-five years age.

TRUTH

...it is not found in names...

When it was time to name their firstborn, a husband and wife began to quarrel. She wanted to name him after her father; he wanted to name him after his. They finally had recourse to the rabbi to settle their dispute.

"What was the name of your father?" the rabbi asked the husband.

"Abijah."

"And what was your father's name?" he asked his wife.

"Abijah."

"Then what's the problem?" said the confused rabbi.

"You see, rabbi," said the woman, "my father was a scholar and his father was a horse-thief. How can I allow my son to be named after a man like that?"

The rabbi gave this very serious thought for the problem was indeed a delicate one. He did not want one party to feel it had won and the other that it had lost. So he finally said, "This is what I suggest you do. Call the boy Abijah. Then wait and see if he becomes a scholar or a horse-thief, and you will know after whom he was named."

221

...or in symbols...

"**I**'m told you sold your bicycle."

"I did."

"How much did you sell it for?"

"Thirty dollars."

"That's a reasonable price."

"It is. But if I had known that the man wasn't going to pay me I would have charged him twice as much."

...in theories.

A manager, who had just returned from a Motivation Seminar, called an employee into his office and said, "henceforth you are going to be allowed to plan and control your job. That will raise productivity considerably, I am sure."

"Will I be paid more?" asked the worker.

"No, no. Money is not a motivator and you will get no satisfaction from a salary raise."

"Well, if production does increase, will I be paid more?"

"Look," said the manager. "You obviously do not understand the motivation theory. Take this book home and read it: it explains what it is that really motivates you."

As the man was leaving, he stopped and said, "If I read this book will I be paid more?"

A couple did not know what to do about the jealousy of their three-year-old son towards the new baby. They were enlightened by a Book of Child Psychology.

One day when the little fellow was in a particularly bad mood the mother said, "Take this teddy bear, son, and show me how you feel towards baby."

According to the Book he was supposed to punch and squeeze the teddy bear. But the three-year-old grabbed the teddy bear by the leg and, with obvious delight, went over to the baby and hit her on the head with it.

...or in words...

"I long to learn spirituality," said a neighbour to Mulla Nasruddin. "Would you come over to my house and talk to me about it?"

Nasruddin did not commit himself. He saw that the man did, indeed, have a spark of intelligence above the average, but he also realized that he was under the delusion that mysticism can be transmitted to another by word of mouth.

Some days later the neighbour called from his roof, "Mullah, I need your help to blow my fire. The embers are going out."

"Why, of course," said Nasruddin. "My breath is at your disposal. Come over to my house and you can have as much of it as you can take away."

* * *

A conductor was rehearsing with his orchestra and said to the trumpet player, "I think this part calls for a more Wagnerian approach, if you get what I mean, something more assertive, so to speak, more accentuated, with more body, more depth, more..."

The trumpet player interrupted. "Do you want it louder, sir?"

All that the poor conductor could say was, "Yes, that's what I mean!"

....in slogans

A religious group was in the habit of using, for its many conferences, a hotel whose motto was written in large words over the walls of the lobby: THERE ARE NO PROBLEMS. ONLY OPPORTUNITIES.

A man approached the hotel desk and said, "Excuse me, I have a problem."

The desk clerk said, with a smile, "We have no problems here, sir. Only opportunities."

"Call it what you want," said the man impatiently. "There's a woman in the room assigned to me."

...in labels

An Englishman migrated to the United States and became an American citizen.

When he went back to England for a vacation one of his relatives reprimanded him for changing his citizenship.

"What have you gained by becoming an American citizen?" she asked him.

"Well, for one thing. I win the American Revolution," was the answer.

...in conventions...

When the Russian-Finnish boundary line was being redrawn a farmer was told that the border passed right through the middle of his land. He therefore had the option of having his land taken into Russia or Finland. He promised to give the matter serious thought; and after some weeks announced that he wanted to live in Finland. A host of incensed Russian officials descended on him to explain the advantages of belonging to Russia, not Finland.

The man heard them out, then said, "I am in complete agreement with everything you say. In fact, it has always been my desire to live in Mother Russia. But at my age I simply won't be able to survive another of those Russian winters."

TRUTH

...or distinctions.

A man was doing his Ph. D in philosophy. His wife realised how seriously he was taking his studies only on the day she said to him, "Why is it you love me so much?"

Quick as a shot he replied, "When you say 'so much' are you referring to intensity, depth, frequency, quality or duration?"

By dissecting her petals
no one ever gathered in
the beauty of the rose.

Nor is it generally found in statistics...

Nasruddin was arrested and taken to court on the charge that he was stuffing horsemeat into the chicken cutlets he served at his restaurant.

Before passing sentence the judge wanted to know in what proportion he was mixing horsemeat with chicken flesh. Nasruddin said, on oath, "It was fifty-fifty, your Honour."

After the trial a friend asked what exactly "fifty-fifty" meant. Said Nasruddin, "One horse to one chicken."

A group of a hundred lumberjacks worked in the forest for six months and two women did their cooking and laundry for them. At the end of that period two of the men married the two women. What the local newspaper said was that two per cent of the men married a hundred per cent of the women.

in logic...

The huge man was preparing to leave the tavern at ten.

"Why so early?" asked the barman.

"Because of the wife."

"So you too are scared of your wife! Are you a man or a mouse?"

"Of one thing I am absolutely sure: I am not a mouse. Because my wife is afraid of mice."

A professor of philosophy in Paris one day declared himself the greatest man in the would and proceeded to prove it to his students in the following fashion:

"Which is the greatest nation on earth?"

"France, of course," they all declared.

"And which is the greatest city in France?"

"Paris, obviously."

"And is not the greatest and holiest place in all Paris its university? And who can doubt that the greatest, the noblest department in any university is its department of philosophy? And, tell me, who is the head of the philosophy department?"

"You," they said in chorus."

Doctor: "That pain in your leg is caused by old age."

Patient: Don't take me for a fool! The other leg is just as old."

232

...or in abstraction...

A disciple said to the Zen Master Hogen, "When I was studying with my previous Master I got some insight in to what Zen is all about."

"So what is this insight you have?" asked Hogen.

"When I asked the Master who Buddha was (by which, of course, I meant Reality), he said. 'Ping-ting comes for fire.'"

"That was a fine reply," said Hogen, "but I fear you may have got it wrong. Tell me what meaning you gave to his words."

"Well," said the disciple, "Ping-ting is the god of fire. Now to say that the god of fire comes for fire is as absurd as to have me, whose true nature is really Buddha, ask who the Buddha is. How can one who is actually, even though unconsciously, the Buddha, formulate a question regarding the Buddha?"

"Ah, ah!" said Hogen. "Exactly what I feared! You're completely off the mark. Now you ask me."

"Very well. Who is Buddha?"

"Ping-ting comes for fire," said Hogen.

The great Gensha once invited a court official to tea. After the customary greetings the official said, "I do not wish to squander this opportunity of spending sometime in the presence of so great a Master. Tell me, what does it mean when they say that in spite of our having it in our daily life we do not see it?"

Gensha offered the man a piece of cake. Then he served him his tea. After eating and drinking, the official, thinking that the Master had not heard his first sentence, repeated the question. "Yes, of course," said the Master. "This is what it means: that we do not see it even though we have it in our daily life."

Those who know, do not say
those who say, do not know.
The wise are therefore silent.
The clever speak—the stupid argue.

TRUTH

Truth has a way of changing.

A passenger was completely lost between the decks of a great Atlantic liner.

He finally ran into a steward and asked for help in finding his cabin.

"What was the number of your cabin, sir?" asked the steward.

"I couldn't tell you, but I'd know it at once, because it had a lighthouse outside the porthole."

Judge: "What's your age."

Convict: "Twenty-two sir."

Judge: "That's what you've been telling us for the last ten years."

Convict: "That's right, sir. I'm not the type that says one thing today and another tomorrow."

Old actress: "I really don't know my age. I keeps changing from minute to minute."

It can be relative.

An American tourist was travelling abroad for the first time. On arrival at his first foreign airport he was faced with a choice between two passageways, one of which was market CITIZENS and the other ALIENS.

He promptly headed for the first one. When told later that he would have to stand in the other line, he protested, "But I'm no alien. I'm an American!"

When the English playwright Oscar Wilde arrived at his club late at night after witnessing the first presentation of a play that had been a complete failure, someone asked, "How did your play go tonight, Oscar?"

"Oh," said Wilde, "the play was a great success. The audience was a failure."

TRUTH

It is concrete...

A monk once said to Fuketsu:

"There is something I heard you say once that puzzled me, namely, that truth can be communicated without speaking and without keeping silent. Would you explain this please?"

Fuketsu replied:

"When I was a lad in South China, ah! how the birds sang among the blossoms in the springtime!"

I think,
therefore I am unconscious
At the moment of thought
I dwell in the UNREAL world
of abstraction
or-of the past
or of the future.

...yet immeasurable.

A frog had lived all his life in a well. One day he was surprised to see another frog there.

"Where have you come from?" he asked.

"From the sea. That's where I live," said the other.

"What's the sea like? Is it big as my well?"

The sea frog laughed. "There's no comparison," he said.

The well frog pretended to be interested in what his visitor had to say about the sea. But he thought, "Of all the liars I have known in my lifetime, this one is undoubtedly the greater—and the most shameless!"

How does one speak of the Ocean
to a frog in the well:
or of Reality
to the ideologue?

Truth is really something you do.

The disciples of Baal Shem once said, "Tell us, dear Rabbi, how we should serve God."

He replied, "How should I know?" ...then went on to tell them the following story:

A king had two friends who were found guilty of crime and sentenced to death. Now even though the king loved them he dared not acquit them outright for fear of giving a bad example to the people. So this is the verdict he gave: A rope was to be stretched across a deep chasm and each of the two men was to walk over it—to safety and freedom or, if he fell, to his death. The first of the two got across safely. The other shouted to the first across the chasm, "Tell me, friend, how you managed it." The first shouted back, "How should I know? All I did was this: When I found myself listing to one side, I leaned to the other."

You don't learn to ride a bicycle in a classroom.

Little boy to the electrician: "What exactly is electricity?"

"I really do not know, son. But I can make it give you light."

A man asked Bayazid to take him on as a disciple.

"If what you seek is Truth," said Bayazid, "there are requirements to be fulfilled and duties to be discharged."

"What are these?"

"You will have to draw water and chop wood and do the housecleaning and cooking."

"I am in search of Truth, not employment," said the man, as he walked away.

Soon after the death of Rabbi Mokshe, Rabbi Mendel of Kotyk asked one of his disciples, "What did your teacher give the greatest importance to?"

The disciple gave it a moment's reflection, then said, "To whatever he happened to be doing at the moment."

It is best expressed in silence.

Bodhidharma is considered the first Zen Patriarch. He was the man who took Buddhism from India to China in the sixth century. When he decided to return home, he gathered his Chinese disciples around him so he could appoint someone to succeed him. He put their powers of perception to the test by asking each of them this question: "What is truth?"

Dofuku said: "Truth is what is beyond affirmation and negation." Bodhidharma said, "You have my skin."

The nun Soji said, "It is like Anand's vision of Buddhaland—glimpsed in a flash, once and forever." Bodhidharma said, "You have my flesh."

Doiku said, "The four elements of wind, water, earth and fire are empty. Truth is no-thing." Bodhidharma replied, "You have my bones."

Finally the Master looked at Eka who bowed law, smiled, and remained silent. Bodhidharma said, "You have my marrow."

The fifth Zen Patriarch, Hung-jun chose Hui-neng from among five hundred monks to be his successor. When asked why, he replied, "The other four hundred and ninety-nine showed a perfect grasp of Buddhism. Huineng alone has no understanding of it whatsoever. He's the type of man that ordinary standards will not measure. So the mantle of authentic transmission has fallen on him."

...and calls for that most formidable accomplishment of the human spirit: an open mind...

The story has it that when New Mexico became part of the United States and the first court session opened in the new state, the presiding judge was a hardened old former cowboy and Indian fighter.

He took his place on the bench and the case opened. A man was charged with horse-stealing. The case for the prosecution was made, the plaintiff and his witnesses were duly heard.

Whereupon the attorney for the defendant stood up and said, "And now, your Honour, I should like to present my client's side of the case."

Said the judge, "Sit down. That won't be necessary. It would only confuse the jury!"

If you have one watch
you know the time.
If you have two watches
you're never sure

...and a fearless heart

𝕿here was a loud knocking in the seeker's heart.

"Who's there?" asked the frightened seeker.

"It is I, Truth," came the answer.

"Don't be ridiculous," said the seeker. "Truth speaks in silence."

That effectively stopped the knocking—to the seeker's great relief.

What he did not know was that the knocking was produced by the fearful beating of his heart.

*The Truth that sets us free is almost always
the Truth we would rather not hear.*

*So when we say something isn't true what we all too frequently
mean is: "I do not like it."*

Its clarity need not be dimmed by politeness...

Rejection slip of a Chinese publishing house that returns a manuscript to its author:

"We have perused your manuscript with exceptional relish. We fear, however, that if we were to publish your outstanding work, it would be quite impossible for us to ever again publish another work that would not come up to its standard. And we cannot imagine how any other work will be its equal in the next hundred years. So, to our deepest regret, we are compelled to return your incredible composition. And we beg you a thousand times over to pardon our shortsightedness and faintheartedness."

...and cultural modes of expression.

An American girl taking dancing lessons in an old-time dancing school showed a constant tendency to lead her partner. This often brought protests like, "Hey! Who's doing the leading—you or me?"

One day her dancing partner happened to be a Chinese lad, who, a few minutes after the dancing began, whispered politely, "Is it not generally more advantageous if, in the dancing process, the lady avoids all preconceived ideas about the direction in which the couple should move?"

It is sometimes concealed by truthfulness...

Two travelling salesmen meet on the platform of a railway station.

"Hello."

"Hello."

Silence.

"Where are you off to?"

"Calcutta."

Silence.

"Listen! When you say you're going to Calcutta, you know that I'll think that you are actually going to Bombay. But I happen to know that you are going to Calcutta. So why don't you tell me truth?"

and sometimes revealed by lies...

A drunk wandering through the city streets at night fell into a cesspool. As he sank deeper into the liquid mess, he began to shout, "Fire, fire, fire!"

Several passersby heard him and came rushing to the rescue. After they had pulled him out they asked why he had shouted "Fire!" when there had been no fire.

He gave them this classic response, "Would any of you have come to the rescue if I had shouted, 'Shit!'?"

A soldier was rushed back home from the front because his father was dying. An exception was made for him because he was all the family his father had.

When he walked into the Intensive Care Ward he suddenly saw that this semi-conscious old man with tubes coming out of him wasn't his father. Someone had made a colossal mistake and rushed back the wrong man.

"How much longer does he have to live?" he asked the doctor.

"Not more than a few hours. You've only just made it."

The soldier thought of this dying man's son fighting God knew where thousands of miles away. He thought of the old man holding on to life in the hope of being with his son one last time before he died. Then he made up his mind. He leaned forward, held the old man's hand and said softly, "Dad, I'm here. I'm back."

The dying man clutched at the hand offered to him; his unseeing eyes opened to scan the surroundings; a contented smile spread over his face and remained there till he died about an hour later.

...but always at one's risk.

A car accident occurred in a small town. A crowd surrounded the victim so a newspaper reporter couldn't manage to get close enough to see him.

He hit upon an idea. "I'm the father of the victim!" he cried. "Please let me through."

The crowd let him pass so he was able to get right up to the scene of the accident and discover, to his embarrassment, that the victim was a donkey.